Praise of M

"If you are   lled
with great i
Melvin Pov
Original Pu

"This book   ster
then you eve
Brian Tracy
Author and

"Ken Hayas   ven
that ANYO   he
knows. Ken   ves.
I'm convinc
Daren Falte
Contributin

"His insights   in-
cial success a   ied
it to simple,   ta-
tions. Ken H
Richard Her
Publisher—

"Here Hayas
Asha Tyson
National Best-selling Author—'How I Retired at 26!'

MILLIONAIRE BY 26

MILLIONAIRE BY 26

✦

Secrets to Becoming A Young, Rich
Entrepreneur

Ken Hayashi

iUniverse, Inc.
New York Lincoln Shanghai

MILLIONAIRE BY 26
Secrets to Becoming A Young, Rich Entrepreneur

Copyright © 2003 by Ken Hayashi

iUniverse books may be ordered through booksellers or by contacting:

iUniverse
2021 Pine Lake Road, Suite 100
Lincoln, NE 68512
www.iuniverse.com
1-800-Authors (1-800-288-4677)

The contents of this book are solely the opinions of the author. It is sold with the understanding that the author is not engaged in rendering legal, accounting or other professional advice. Always seek professional financial and legal counsel before making financial decisions.

The Author disclaims any personal liability, loss or risk incurred as a consequence of the use and application, either directly of indirectly, of any advice, information, or methods presented in this publication.

ISBN-13: 978-0-595-28080-3
ISBN-10: 0-595-28080-3

Printed in the United States of America

Contents

Acknowledgments

Countless people have intentionally or unintentionally taught me the keys to success. My techniques, philosophies, mistakes and successes have been formulated through interacting with the greatest teachers.

Many contributors, including Lance Murkin, Terry Thomas and Daren Falter assisted me with the marketing research. To my mentors Anthony Robbins, Robert Kiyosaki and Donald Trump who helped me with my focus. Cliff Carle for taking my swirl of ideas and techniques and organized them into this book. And my sincere thanks go to Franklin Chiu, William Higa, Felix Gil, Howard Oberstein, Warren Meyer, Jim Fahrenholz and Melvin Powers.

And to those people in my life who have so skillfully used their illusion of power to tell me what they thought was impossible, played their games of manipulation, and caused me much pain. I thank you so much for supplying me with the inspiration and overwhelming drive that created Millionaire By 26.

Thank you to my wife Somruthai, for her insights and encouragement that gave me strength when events sometimes felt hopeless. And to my daughters Alexis and Ashley for showing me the greatest courage by overcoming major unforeseen obstacles. Finally, I would like to thank my parents Shigeru and Tsuyako, for always encouraging me by letting me know that "I can achieve and become anything I wanted in life."

Introduction

DO YOU WANT TO BE A MILLIONAIRE?

Wouldn't it be great to find out one week that your state has been trying to locate the latest lotto winner? Some lucky person never came up to claim their prize, and you realize, "Wait a minute, I never checked my ticket." Imagine you were to find out that you had all six numbers and you are the newest millionaire. Or you got on one of those Reality or Game Shows, and you've been narrowed down to one of the final contestants. The next thing you know, the host is presenting you with a million dollar check.

It seems everyone is on this millionaire craze. People all across the country are dreaming of one day becoming a millionaire. They are either glued to the television imagining themselves as the contestant playing for a million dollar prize, or they're buying lotto tickets religiously, or of course everyone's favorite, hoping to hit the big jackpot in Las Vegas.

Millionaire By 26 is about the real truth. It introduces students and young adults to the world of entrepreneurs, start-ups, and home-based businesses that eventually grew into multimillion dollar ventures. And it's about how you too can apply simple everyday techniques to reach financial independence, beyond your wildest dreams.

Millionaire By 26 also includes...

- Three essential techniques you will absolutely need to master in order to become financially independent.

- Why listening to the *right people* is a key to creating and maintaining wealth.

- How you can get millionaires to talk to you for hours about their life and their secret strategies.

- How to start and/or select the right business in the right industry at the right time.

- Strategies on how to evaluate moneymaking opportunities such as infomercials, mail-order, multilevel marketing (the difference between legitimate moneymaking programs verses the deceptive ones).

- How you can turn your current job into a stepping stone to your financial independence—even if it is a "dead end job."

- How to take control of your in-and-out cash flow once you have started your home-based business.

- What you can learn from a reality show such as *The Apprentice*.

- And finally, how your one-person, home-based business operation can grow and lead you to that illusive goal: Financial Independence.

1

Simple, But Very Effective

In martial arts, you can defeat an attacker regardless of his size or strength, with ONE MOVE. My program to get you on the path toward making a million dollars or more uses a simple principle. Most people believe that you need to learn a vast number of "secret techniques" to defend yourself or to become financially independent. But, learning a bunch of fancy moves and "Hollywood kicks" or just wanting to learn a host of "inside secrets" on amassing personal wealth, will usually amount to someone who is all show and no substance. This book is not designed to load you up with a huge array of financial secrets and techniques. It avoids such hype as "the hottest new secrets that'll have you rich beyond your wildest dreams overnight!" Rather, it is skillfully designed to show you that you only need to master a few simple and basic techniques in order to become RICH.

Who Are You?

You are a young, eager individual who knows that you want to have financial independence but don't know how to do it—or even where to start. And you don't just hope for it, but you're willing to do something toward obtaining it. You are someone who wants more from life. You even dare to want to be your own boss. Maybe you have always done what your parents told you to do, but now you see that there might be another way of doing things. Maybe you have just gotten out of high school or college, or you have dropped out of college and entered the workforce. Did you manage to get a job in the field you majored in, or are you at least working in an area that interest you?

You might be worried about the stability of your job or worried that there may not be a job waiting for you when you complete school. You don't want to end up like perhaps your parents, or aunts and uncles, or other older people you know. They are in their 40s, 50s, or 60s, and they're still struggling to make ends meet, or are wondering if they'll have enough money for retirement. They give you career advice, but they don't have the answers—otherwise they'd be rich. So why should you listen to them?

You have seen those infomercials on television about moneymaking opportunities. You have read articles about the kid who had a great idea and became a millionaire overnight. Maybe someone has approached you from a marketing company offering a moneymaking potential that seemed too good to be true. Was it really too good to be true, or could this be the path to success? You are asking yourself if these programs are for real. Do people really make the kind of money that these programs claim? How can you know what works and what doesn't?

The fact that you've asked yourself these questions means that you are already on your way to financial success. You have come to a realization that most people never do—that working for someone else is not the answer. You haven't waited until you're in your 40s and are laid off to realize that there are opportunities out there just waiting for you. And you have an advantage over those older people who are just now trying to grab at independence and financial success. You're young, and you have the energy to go full speed ahead toward success. You can use that natural energy and drive to achieve your goals.

Let me tell you a little about myself. In brief, I generated over a million dollars in business then "retired" at age 26. I worked with several sales and marketing companies in the past and was a top earner for them. I've always made six figures, but recently, I have been working for *myself*. While it involves much more risk and responsibility being my own boss, I've never been happier. I don't have a new invention or a Pet Rock. I'm not an athlete or a celebrity, and I didn't start an Internet company and made a killing on an IPO before the bubble burst. I don't even have a college degree.

To reach the income level I've achieved, I have used some simple, but very effective techniques that I am going to teach you throughout this program. Please consider this book a workshop to get you on track for financial independence. I will give you the tools that you can apply to *any* industry so that you can succeed. This will have nothing to do with luck.

The techniques I will teach you in this program can be applied toward anything you want to do. For example just utilizing the *three simple techniques,* laid out in Chapters 4–7, can give you the confidence to know that you will be able to succeed in any industry you wish to pursue, just as it has done for me. I have mastered these techniques, and I will show you how you can master them through the course of this program.

Why am I Sharing the Secrets?

You are probably wondering why I am sharing this knowledge. I believe that in creating this program, I am providing a service to a generation that has been ignored by most other programs designed to help people achieve success. I am actually still kind of naïve because it hasn't been that long since I generated my first million. I still have a lot of enthusiasm and I still feel that I am inexperienced in life. This is my first time making real money. But even though I don't possess vast knowledge, I know what it's like to be young, with the motivation to achieve financial success. What I feel I can do that no one else has done is to motivate you, the younger generation, to use your energy and drive to be successful.

Have you ever listened to a couple of talking heads on CNN or attempted to decipher what your professor was telling you in a math or business class you had taken? I had an extremely difficult time trying to take some of the information that they were providing and apply it to my life.

If you are in a trade, college or high school right now, let's say you are taking a math or an accounting class. You read the textbook for the class cover to cover. You memorize certain definitions. You are now able to shoot out answers that the professor asks you regarding a formula. But, is that book going to lead you to financial success? It's possible—but probably not. There are plenty of people who will make an 'A' in the class, yet will not understand the fundamentals of acquiring personal wealth, even though the information was contained in the book they studied in order to take their tests and quizzes. The problem is, information is seldom presented in a practical and applicable way. All too often these classes dispense hypothetical information without giving you the means to process it, in the real world.

Recently, I reviewed programs produced by Forbes Magazine called, "Great Minds of Business." In it, they have interviews with entrepreneurs, CEOs of companies such as FedEx and Intel, and the former chairman of the Federal Reserve. Some of them are millionaires and some of them are billionaires. But they cater to older generations. Andrew Grove, CEO of Intel, talks about what an avid reader he is, and how he's read such and such, listing a host of authors I've never even heard of, let alone read. He speaks of techniques he uses with his teams to increase profitability in his multibillion dollar company. But these are techniques that neither you nor I can apply to our present situation.

I've also reviewed "The Warren Buffet Portfolio." But the last time Mr. Buffet was middle income or in the financial situation that you may be in now, was when he was in his 20s, and that was back in the early part of last century. Information that he gives today on managing your personal wealth may not be as relevant to you as it is to someone in a much higher tax bracket.

But don't get me wrong, I do get a lot out of these programs. However, as I said, I can't always relate to what they say because they're generally aimed at an older generation. Therefore I have aimed this book at the younger generation by making it "younger-user" friendly. I will not delve into some philosophy on how the Federal Reserve needs to allocate funds for future financial crisis, or how to analyze statistical calculations to attempt to lower millions of dollars in operating costs to make a 1% profit in a billion dollar company. You'll get none of that kind of information. I can tell you right now, in order to become a millionaire it is absolutely not necessary to know or understand that type of trivial information. Yes, it can be helpful, but it's simply not necessary and I will not waste your time with arcane financial philosophies. If you have had to study diverse theories on business or finance and found yourself asking, "What does *that* have anything to do with me? I just want to know the fastest legal way to be rich," then this book is for you! I'm not going to give you lofty, over-the-top information you can't relate to, because if you can't relate to something, it's much more difficult to process it.

Information Versus Application

Let's say you are not exceptionally articulate. When you walk into a crowded room, you do not have the party swooning over you because they're intoxicated by your exquisite command of the English language. Would reading a dictionary or a thesaurus cover to cover make you more articulate? Mostly, what it would do is give you information without giving you the means to process it. It certainly wouldn't be a user-friendly way of becoming a great conversationalist and communicator. To do that, you or I would need to learn the techniques and the processes to *apply* the words to speech.

This is my intention for this book: I am going to *ease* you into an understanding of the *secret* to success. What you'll learn is a condensed version of what I learned through my process—and the secret is that *there's no secret at all*. You only think it's a big secret because even though it might be staring you in the face, you don't know yet how to recognize it, understand it and process it. This program is going to help you to decode that so-called "secret."

I won't be giving you a lot of materials in this program. I keep it simple by showing you brief and basic techniques. Once you have mastered these techniques, it's time to "graduate" and move on. I worked out these techniques by studying personal development and personal finance programs that cater to older generations and then retooled them to apply to the people of my generation. Many of these programs gave philosophical instead of practical information. They were too sophisticated and didn't apply to my financial situation when I first listened to them. They were aimed at people who had already lost their dreams and were desperate to regain them. They catered to people who had already married, had kids, had careers, had mortgages, perhaps divorced, were paying alimony, or were retired and worrying about their stock portfolios. These programs wanted to shake these people up and tell them that life was still possible. Some even showed people how to increase their energy so they could get their dreams back and have the drive to achieve them. They had very little to do with me.

I was still creating my dream, and I had limitless energy and a long future ahead of me. So I took the philosophies these programs gave older people and I turned them into techniques that I could use to become successful. I had an advantage that those older people didn't by having a clear path to achieve my dream and the drive and energy to do it. You have that too, so let me help you take advantage of that.

As you go through this workshop, you'll learn the importance of coaches or mentors. I listened to the personal development series from Nightingale Conant and Tony Robbins' tapes, and I used them as *kinds of coaches*. These tapes didn't substitute for real coaches, but they had value for me and I got a lot out of them. But let me talk for a minute about Tony Robbins, who I think is a great coach and mentor.

The first Tony Robbins tape program I listened to was *Personal Power 1*. He recorded this back in the mid 1980s when he was 29 years old and had made his first million dollars. He sounded young and enthusiastic as he talked about how he used to make $38,000 a year and now had a net worth of over $1,000,000. The attitude and excitement he had rang in his voice and were captured on that tape.

The programs he has now are more refined and his techniques are more targeted and focused. Tony Robbins is in his 40s now, and his tone seems much more sophisticated and kind of relaxed. The tape he made when he was 29 resonates a lot stronger for me than these newer tapes, because I can relate much better to the "still hungry" person he was back then. But please don't get me wrong—I'm not saying that I think his newer tapes are bad or do not have as much information. In fact, they have *more* information and his newer techniques are more refined. But when I listen to his earlier tapes, I can understand the struggles he went through because I have gone through them myself very recently. This is why I think that what I have to say to you will make sense to you.

If I were writing this in my 30s or 40s, I'm sure my attitude would be different than it is now. It's not that long ago that I was getting out of high school and wondering what I was going to do with my life, but if I talked about that when I was in my 40s it would be as mismatched as those 40-year-old writers who do sitcoms about life in today's high schools. It would be a little off the mark. When I reach my 30s and 40s, my priorities will have changed, as yours will. But right now I can relate to your priorities, because they're mine, too.

Today, when I go out to dinner with friends, I don't have to look at the right side of the menu and decide what I'm going to order by how much it will cost. But this is the first time in my life that I can do this, so I know very vividly what it's like to be broke, because it wasn't very long ago that I had no money. The last time Andrew Grove or Warren Buffet had to worry about the prices on a menu was probably 50 or 60 years ago. Most of what they have to say now is for an older audience. What I have to say is for you.

I experienced what you're experiencing now just a couple years ago. I have recently felt what you're feeling now, so I believe that I can communicate the techniques to make you successful at your age better than someone who is too far away from the experience of having the dream, the drive, and the energy all at once. It was only a year or so ago that I'd answer the phone and a telemarketer would ask for Mr. Hayashi. I'd say, "Yes?" and they'd say, "No, I need to speak to the *man* of the house, please." I still sound like a kid sometimes, and you might, too. So use me as your stepping stone to the programs for older people, because I'll give you the foundation aimed at your age that probably no one else is offering.

It will probably take you about a week to go through this program, but it might take more than a year for you to truly master each of the techniques. I might be a slow learner, because it took me over five years to master these three techniques. But while I was doing that, I was studying other people as well, and it was sometimes too much information to absorb. This is why I am giving you the benefit of my experience, with you, the eager, energetic young dreamer in mind.

I am by no means the most successful young entrepreneur around. There are plenty of young entrepreneurs out there who make more money than I do and who have sold their companies for over hundreds of millions dollars. They may be interviewed in articles, or giving speeches about what they've done, but they aren't creating programs offering you their techniques in a simple step by step method. So I am stepping up to fill that need. I am giving you a targeted, basic-but-essential foundation so you can build something—anything. I am also going to do my best to make sure you are inspired, as I was to move in the direction you want to go.

2

Who Do You Listen To?

Who Do You Listen To?

This is the first question you need to ask yourself. And this is something that will come up repeatedly, no matter what type of industry you are in. One of the first questions asked of me by an entrepreneur who happened to be a millionaire was, "Do you want to make over $100,000 this year?" My answer to that question was "yes," and I was extremely serious about my answer.

So what is the first thing that I should be doing to accomplish this? Well, the first thing is that I should be listening to people who are making at least $100,000 a year, because they obviously know what they're doing. Even though this is a very simple answer, it takes many people a long time to understand this. Some people will say that the question is silly and the answer is no secret. They might say, "I want to know how to become wealthy, and you are not teaching me how to become wealthy." But you need to know what question to ask first, whom to ask that question of, and then how to act on their answer.

Who Shouldn't You Listen To?

Everyone has a friend who knows everything about car repairs. Let's call your friend Bob. Bob can pinpoint what's wrong with a car just by starting it up. He can immediately tell if there's a problem with the transmission, the fuel injector, the valves, or whatever. Bob is the guy you turn to when you have a problem with your car, or when you want to buy a used car, or even when a mechanic tells you something needs to be done on your car and you'll feel better having a second opinion. But what if you had a question about your taxes? Would you ask Bob for tax advice?

To ask that question seems ridiculous. But this is the kind of thing people do, day in and day out. They decide that they want to become wealthy, but they turn to people who are not qualified to give them advice. They ask Bob, or their drinking buddies, co-workers, best friends, classmates, or in some cases teachers. They're not asking the appropriate people, so they can't get the correct answer.

I mentioned that teachers aren't the ones to give you advice on how to get wealthy, and some of you might be offended by that. You might know a teacher or have a relative who is a teacher—either in high school, trade school, or college. And teachers deserve respect because of what they do—educate—but only a few of them know how to become wealthy. In fact, most teachers are always struggling to get their wages increased and better benefits. Once again, don't get me wrong—I'm not putting down teachers—I'm just saying to be sure that if you choose a teacher as a mentor, be sure he or she is truly *financially* savvy.

So the first thing to make sure you understand is that you need to listen to advice from the appropriate person—a *financially successful* mentor. If the question you want to ask is, "How do I start making $100,000 a year?" then you have to ask the right person or the answer you get will not be correct. As you accomplish that goal and you increase the number up to $200,000, $300,000, $500,000, $1 million a year or even $10 million a year, you need to make sure that you are always seeking advice from the appropriate mentor.

Where Do You Find a Mentor?

Some people will say, "Those kinds of people are not around me. I don't know people who make that kind of money that I can ask." The reality is that there are plenty of people all around for you to ask and listen to. All you need to do is open your eyes and look for them. Look at all the businesses around you. Not all of them are owned by major corporations. Many of them are owned by entrepreneurs who live in your city. You can meet those entrepreneurs, develop a friendship with them, and have them become your mentors.

You can choose to have new friends in your life. You don't have to be limited to those friends that you went to grade school with. You can develop new friends who are successful millionaires and can help you. They don't even have to be your own age.

How Do You Develop the Relationship?

Some people will argue with me about this, saying, "Those people don't want to talk to me. I went and asked a successful entrepreneur for advice, and he didn't want to give me any." I then ask them, "How long after you met them did you ask for advice?"

How long does it take to build a friendship with a best friend or significant other? Maybe you hit it off with someone immediately, but it usually takes time for a friendship to grow. How long was it until you felt you trusted a friend enough to reveal your secrets? Why should a business owner be any different than you are? He has a "secret" that you want to know—information that could make you wealthy. But you have to build a relationship first.

If the first question out of your mouth is, "How did you become a millionaire?" Can you blame him or her if they take offense and may not wish to talk to you? Instead, get to know the entrepreneur the way you would any friend. Build trust over time. Most business owners are just regular people, like you and me, and they're not going to share their information until they know you and feel comfortable about you.

I personally enjoy going to seminars and attending business organization meetings. Years ago, after college, I made it an effort to attend local business presentations. I was at this particular one and usually they had a speaker. During those days telecom was hot. You might remember all those 10/10 commercials, or telemarketers calling your parents and offering low long distance, and phone companies popping up left and right. This came to fruition right along side the Internet boom.

Anyway, at this meeting, the speaker was an owner of a small telecom company that had just below 30 people in it. He was making about $40,000 a month. Back then, I thought that was an enormous amount of money, being I was broke. I was nervous at first going up to him to just talk with him. But, I said, "Hello, I enjoyed your presentation." Yes the first encounter was brief. But I discovered when and where his other speaking engagements were, and I made a point to attend them. About the third time that he saw that I was attending each of his seminars, he was very receptive when I asked him if he could show me how he built up his company. He saw that I looked up to him as an expert in his field, and that I just wanted information.

Later on, I was invited to spend a day at his company, which was difficult because I was working at the time. But I wasn't going to let this opportunity pass me by. I met his staff and just as human beings are, eventually a friendship grew and I learned more and more on how to build companies. This eventually helped me to launch my entrepreneurial ventures.

A similar scenario should be happening with you. I do not play golf or tennis, so I am not a member of a country club. I attended local business meetings. This is a great way to start. Examples are Chamber of Commerce, City Council, Toast Masters or business presentations advertised in the business sections of your local paper. However, if on your off hours you are spending your time at your local sports bar, it will be unlikely that a millionaire mentor is going to saunter up to you and say, "Would you like to learn what I have to teach?"

Mentors By Interning

Another opportunity that people often overlook is to become an intern. If you're currently going to school, it's a perfect opportunity to spend two or three days out of the week interning at a company. Or immediately after graduating, intern at a company or industry that you wish to pursue. If you are already working, this may be difficult. However, rather than take a second job, consider becoming an intern so you can learn. Generally speaking, there is a freedom that you may have as a student because of fewer financial responsibilities. Take advantage of this time in your life.

What I see a lot of people do is as soon as they graduate, it to start looking for work. They are thinking, "How much can I get paid an hour? How much is this company going to pay me annually? What kind of benefits will I get?" If you are already beginning to ask questions like this you have already trapped yourself, and have closed your mind to the opportunities available beyond employment.

Interning is a way that you can show your talents and express to a company that you are willing to work hard, look at the long-term, and most importantly, demonstrate to the executive or business owner that you are not there working just to collect a paycheck. Being a business owner myself, I've noticed that when an employee is working for you, they are not always performing at their best. And often, all they are doing is collecting a paycheck every two weeks. They are for-ever dealing with human resources: "Where is my vacation pay? Do I get over-time? Why does she get paid more than me when I've been here longer? Do I get my 6% raise this year?" To an employer, questions like these can be annoying. But if you come to them as an intern, with the mentality, "I am here for *your* ben-efit, and in turn to show you what I can do," that is a breath of fresh air to them.

Let's look at the story of an intern: Sean "P. Diddy" Combs. While very con-troversial for his personal and professional life, it can't be denied he's a very pow-erful individual. Back in the late '80s and early '90s, Sean, in his late teens, loved dancing in hip-hop nightclubs. And at these clubs where he was dancing were scouts who were always looking for talent. He was eventually noticed and was asked to be a back-up dancer in a couple of music videos. While he was on the set of one of these video shoots, he saw and was intrigued by "not the *star* of the video, but the people behind the camera wearing the *suits*." And he decided he wanted to be one of *those* people.

Sean wanted to work for a guy named Andre Herrell, who was starting Uptown Records. Basically, Sean asked to work for Andre as an intern. And the story goes that Andre said, "Work for free? Sounds great! Now, go outside and wash my car." So Sean was working for the company as an intern for six months, when one day, an executive at Uptown left the company. This gave Sean, then a 19-year-old, his big opportunity. He convinced Andre that since Uptown was trying to market to the hip-hop young market and that he himself was a young hip-hop individual, then he, Sean, would be an ideal producer.

He proved himself and was soon recognized in the music industry by producing a couple of artists who hit the charts. Later he was offered the opportunity to start his own production company, Bad Boy, through Arista records. Since then he has become a successful producer, as well as a personally being a hip-hop artist. He also has his own clothing line, and owns a New York restaurant. He was ranked as a Forbes' Under 40, Top 40 Richest Individuals in America.

What Are Other Ways to Find a Mentor?

Okay, so maybe you live in a completely dead town. All the businesses are owned by major corporations, or the town is so small that there are no businesses that make real money. You don't have anybody you can cultivate and then listen to. How do you get a millionaire to talk to you?

The information is still there for you, but it's not in the form of a person who you can have lunch with to ask advice. Instead, you can allow *technology* to help you to get that crucial information. You can hear a millionaire talk for hours about their life and strategies. You can listen to millionaires and billionaires on tapes. And over the course of these tapes, they will answer just about any question you would ask of them.

This is essentially what you are doing right now with this book. And you need to keep on doing it. I always wanted to learn how someone built and maintained a multimillion- or multibillion-dollar empire. How did they take a company public? How did they become a leader in their industry without having a product, service, or invention that was exclusive to their company? What business concepts allow a person to succeed based only on their own innovation and creativity? How did they learn to tap into their own potential?

I recently got some audiotapes by Michael Dell. (By the way, I prefer to listen to tapes because I'm actually a terrible reader and the benefits of reviewing tapes versus books is enormous for me.) On the tapes, he explains how he built up his own company. Dell by no means invented the computer. But he talks about using his innovations and developing a niche market. Listening to these tapes is like meeting with Michael Dell for lunch. At that "lunch," I'm able to "mentally ask" him all the questions I want him to answer for me by simply listening carefully to each word. I am able to get him to "answer" questions about his business for four hours without having to interrogate him.

Would it be realistic for me to expect to have lunch with Michael Dell? Why would he want to meet with me, and would he even have the time to talk with me? Even if I could meet him for lunch, how many questions would I be able to ask him—two or three? How could I possibly get four hours of Michael Dell's time so he could explain everything that was important to his achieving his success?

The answer is it is highly unlikely. But for the price of about $20, I can pick Michael Dell's brain by listening to his audiotape. You can get other tapes by successful people in the industries that interest you. I am interested in business, so from time to time, I hand my credit card to the clerk at Barnes and Noble, and four hours later I have heard a successful entrepreneur tell me about how he or she beat out their opponents to achieve success. What a great school this is for us, being able to receive information on demand. Books written by entrepreneurs maybe great for some people, but you need a quiet place to read, and the uninterrupted time to read them.

Any time I am going to drive anywhere, I listen to audiotapes in my car. I don't listen to music anymore when I drive. My friends see my backseat filled with tapes by business professionals who give me their philosophies on how to bring the best out of myself. How long would it take me to finish a book, and would I ever read a book two or three times? I don't know if I would even finish a book, but I can listen to these tapes over and over as often as I need to. Tapes are better than CDs, because if you take the tape out of your car and wish to continue listening to it at home or with a portable player, the tape has stopped exactly where you left off. CDs currently do not have that option and you will end up spending time rewinding and fast forwarding just to see where you left off. That is time wasted.

These tapes provide me with mentors to follow and study. I don't need to have lunch with a billionaire, because I can listen to a tape and hear what it took someone to be successful, and it's as if it was recorded just for me. These tapes are the bridge between them and you. You don't need to join an exclusive country club to get the inside information on industries and markets. This high-level information is provided to you on tape.

Why Is Listening to the Right People the Key to Creating and Maintaining Wealth?

What I'm going to tell you next is a very basic concept that not only I, but a lot of financial coaches talk about. It's common knowledge to success-oriented people, but this may be new information to you. The basics are very simple: if you want to be successful, you need to listen to successful people. If you want to be a great tennis player, you study great tennis players—not great golfers or football players. You need to surround yourself with great tennis players. It's not likely that they will tell you how bad you are at tennis. They will tell you what's good about you and what you need to improve.

So let's apply this to financial freedom. When it comes to money, everyone has an opinion about it. People can be extremely passionate about it, or understand it, or treat it like the plague. Money can basically be a measurement of a person's value, position or worth to society (similar to a report card). And since it is a measure of your current status in life, it is no wonder that some people can take great offense at discussions of money, and others take great pride in their understanding of it.

How Can Your Friends' Feelings About Money Hurt Your Goals?

If your passion was tennis, even your friends who did not compete in tennis would most likely encourage you to be great at it. However, when it comes to the subject of money, there are generally strong emotions attached to it. Whether they like it or not, people are very touchy about their money. You have absolutely no control over other people's feelings about money. So if you have a friend who isn't in control of their personal finances, they will often discourage you from your goal of financial success. Whether or not they admit it, they aspire to wealth too, and envy anyone who has it. And even if that person is a friend, they might look down on you for your goal of obtaining wealth. They might misinterpret the desire to succeed for greed.

What I am about to say is extremely important. At first it may seem insignificant, or perhaps a given, but if followed rigorously, it can change your life: *Do not listen to negative people.* People with negative opinions about wealth could be relatives, people you love, close friends, or people you have looked up to. They may even be your parents. Whoever they are, it is not their *character* that is negative. They have negative opinions because they have formed a negative emotional attachment to money and will discourage you from obtaining it. Because they don't have money, or cannot pursue or acquire wealth themselves, they may discourage and perhaps even condemn you. Even talking with them about your goal of becoming wealthy will be perceived as an attack on them. Even though they have nothing to do with you or your finances, it will likely be seen as an attack on their relationship with you.

Unfortunately, a majority of the poor and middle class have this kind of mentality. Because of their mindset, they automatically discourage anybody who tries to acquire wealth. They discourage what you do in order to excel. When this happens with someone who is close to you, you need to remember that they are simply letting their own feelings about money come through. Do not allow them to influence you, even though you care about them. They are biased and are not looking out for your best interests and your goals. If they are your family, love them but do not listen to them. However, you have the choice to surround yourself with whomever you choose. Love your family unconditionally, but choose your friends carefully.

The rich surround themselves with others who are rich. They surround themselves with like-minded people who aspire to the same goals. If the people that currently surround you do not aspire to the same goals you do—to become wealthy and successful—it may not be wise to keep them around you. This is because you become like those who surround you.

Some people have heard me say this and feel that it is extremely cruel. I have given you information here that is not exactly what they taught you in school. This is probably not the way your parents raised you to think. And this may not be something that your friends have talked about. But this technique is not a secret. I have not revealed something that only the high society knows about. It is common knowledge among the rich, but even if the poor and middle class have heard this information, they choose not to accept it. They often condemn the rich for keeping the "secret to wealth" from them. And the sad fact is, they also condemn anybody in their peer group who aspires to be rich. Therefore, choose friends who share your goals and support you instead of criticizing you.

Why Do You Need Personal Development Coaches?

Personal development or financial coaches are mentors that you have found locally, a seminar program that you attend weekly or an audiotape program that you listen to regularly. When it comes to personal development coaches, each one has their own interpretation of how to achieve wealth. They come at it from differing angles, and how effective they are all depends on how *you* accept and interpret their information. I don't see any one of them as being more right or wrong. Each one has interpreted information in their own way because of their own life experiences. So one coach will ring truer to someone who has had a similar upbringing and experiences than another coach. Maybe one coach talks about how he was in the Vietnam War, and he tells what happened when he came back looking for a job. This coach will have a stronger impact on someone else who was also in the Armed Services and felt he or she lost out on opportunities while they were serving their time.

But what most success coaches will ask you first, very simply is, "*Where are you now?*" They will make you determine exactly what stage of your life you are in and why you are there. They will have you establish what is most important in your life, because you need to know where you are before you can start down a path to where you want to end up. The next question then is, "*Where do you want to go?*" This is not such a revolutionary question to ask. But in asking this question, the coach starts you on heavy goal-setting exercises that help you to determine *exactly* where you want to go.

The next thing a coach will do is to get you to *take action*. The absolute most important factor in everything is for you to take action on it. Even if the action you take is the wrong one, at least you are moving toward something rather than sitting back and doing nothing. No matter which personal development coach you listen to, they all will tell you that you need to take action—period.

Yes, it's important to know where you are and where you want to go, but regardless of which success coach you study, it's all useless unless you take action, then *follow through* on your actions. And you will see that it's not enough just to take action for a couple of weeks. You must consistently be taking action in order to reach your goal.

There's one final thing that the more advanced coaches talk about. However, if you don't know exactly how to balance this final technique, it can actually be an impediment to your success. This is because many people try to do it too quickly. This final technique is to *evaluate and adjust*. The reason many coaches don't talk about how to evaluate and adjust is that if they don't teach it accurately, or they leave any details out, the student will not interpret it correctly.

Unless they are skillfully taught how to apply this technique, most students will jump right in and start evaluating and adjusting immediately after they take action on their plans. And when that happens, it's basically like not taking action at all. They start checking on themselves a week or even 3 to 4 months after they have taken action. Evaluating and making adjustments too soon stops the action that has barely gotten started. They never really get the ball rolling.

In sum, give your goal a chance to "take roots," to demonstrate to you that it has the potential to grow and eventually succeed. But, after a *reasonable* amount of time (usually six months to a year) if your progress has stagnated or leveled off, *that's* the time to ask yourself, "What could I do *differently* to get back on track for success?"

Michael Dell's Story

Michael Dell founded Dell Computers. His concept of "direct to the top" is a form of direct marketing that eliminates the middleman. He learned this concept when he was only in elementary school by selling stamps through mail order. While he was attending the University of Texas, Dell started building computers in his dorm room.

Back then, the average IBM computer cost $3,000. But Dell knew that if you bought all the computer parts separately, it only cost about $700. So he started bidding on projects to supply schools with computers. It made sense to schools and businesses to buy comparable-quality computers at much more competitive prices from young Michael Dell.

When his freshman dorm room became too small for building computers, he moved to a 1,000-square-foot office. He had three other guys building computers with him and was soon generating $50,000 to $60,000 a month with his business. He dropped out of college after his freshman year to run his business on a full-time basis. He obviously achieved success, because Dell Computers is one of the biggest computer suppliers in the nation. Dell competes with huge companies like IBM. Eventually, he did have to tell his parents that he had dropped out of college.

All of his life, Michael had heard about capitalism and seizing opportunities. His mother was a stockbroker and business was often a subject discussed at the dinner table. He was fortunate to be programmed at an early age to be aware of business, which prepared him to build his own success. Most young people do not have the advantage of hearing about capitalism and business on a daily basis. They don't have the early programming that helps them see opportunities when they present themselves. When young people begin to hear about business for the first time, it's often like a foreign language to them. They are not used to this kind of information and may quickly reject or ignore it. If this has been your experience for most of your early life, you now have the power to begin listening to the appropriate people, and to be able to reprogram your mind to see opportunities, wherever or whenever they present themselves.

The reason I know this story is that for about $20, I bought Michael Dell's tapes and heard him in his own voice explain how he built his company. He has given me pointers on how I can apply his concepts to my own ventures. So while driving in my car, I can have Michael Dell tell me how it all worked for him. You can do the same with the mentor of your choosing and have it work for you, too.

3

What you absolutely NEED to be Rich

What Will It Take?

So you want to be *rich*? If you're reading this book, your answer to this question is obvious: Yes! Yes! And YES! But you're probably thinking, "I do not want to hear some sugarcoated, *unrealistic* 'shortcut to riches.' Nor do I want to hear some mysterious, convoluted philosophy that requires a 180 IQ to decipher. What I *do* want is a technique that is straightforward, makes sense, and I can apply it to *my* life—if you've got something like *that* to help me become rich, count me in!"

I'm not going to B.S. you. I'm not going to tell you that my formula for success is "instant!" I know you're not that foolish. At the same time, I don't pull any punches. You are going to have to do some work. But the good news is, you won't have to work that *hard* just *steady*. An airplane requires a lot of effort to get off the ground. But once it is in flight and on course, it glides almost effortlessly to its destination. If you put in a steady effort, and you stay the course, what may seem like real work in the beginning, will soon become second nature—like you're on automatic pilot—leading you to the results you've always wanted.

In this section I'll tell you exactly what it is going to take on your part. I've noticed that some motivational speakers do not like to say that right up front. That is because it puts the burden on *you*. It puts the responsibility for success directly on your shoulders. But how can any legitimate formula for riches truly work if it doesn't start with you? There is no magic wand that can be waved over your head transforming you into an instant financial genius. So if you go in prepared to do *your part* to become rich, then this information that I am about to present to you will do *it's part* to get you there.

So how do I become rich? Obviously, you would like the answer to be "someone will see your potential and front you the seed money to turn your idea into a million dollar business." Or, the answer we'd all like to hear, "a rich uncle will give you his fortune for you to start your own business." But that is not the answer that I am going to give you. Instead, I'm going to be very realistic—but at the same time, very *optimistic*. Why? Because you are trying to create wealth in a country that will *support* your efforts to do so. A country that has the resources available today to make any (realistic) dream come true. You may have a great idea and not much more. But you, like most other Americans, are aware that there's something more. You know that there is great opportunity because you are living in this country. The American government will allow you to become wealthy, will support you in becoming wealthy, and all you need to know is, "What are the tools that I personally need to make that money?"

Start a Business

What you are going to do is start your own business this week. "What? Start my own business?" you say. "Are you crazy? I never thought about owning my own business. Even if I did, I don't have any money. I thought this book was about how to get rich while you are still young. I don't know the first thing about running my own business. That's all I have to do is own my own company? That was no secret. Who is going to lend me money to start my own business?"

First of all, you do not need to have a lot of money to start your own business. Many entrepreneurs began very small and I will explain some of the options in a minute. So, before we go into the options, let me quickly explain the reasons why. We live in this great country that allows us to be rich. If you want to be rich, you need to start a business. There is no way around it. Starting a business allows us not to just have a great idea or a dream, but to put your ideas to great use with the potential to have huge financial rewards. People did not get rich in this country with just a great idea, it was the *application* of the great idea using some of the techniques covered in this book, that made the idea blossom into a million or a billion dollar venture.

Most personal finance books will all agree, and they will go on for chapters and chapters explaining why you need to start a business. They'll try to convince you that since we live in a capitalistic country you should become a capitalist—it's the land of opportunity, etc. But I am not going to go into long, complicated and analytical reasons why you should start a business. Instead, I am going to assume that you already know that is your main opportunity for wealth. Thinking that you can finish college, get a degree, get the job and within a couple years you're going to be rich, is very unrealistic. Yes, maybe you can do that.

However, there is not enough of a percentage of the people who have successfully done that to support that theory. Yes, some individuals have become rich by working for the right company. And in most instances, this was the result of the company having hired them in its infancy stage. Most likely the company would have recruited people with an entrepreneurial spirit. In essence, everyone was part of a start-up team and they all grew with the business. So you now know step one, you need to start your own business. Big or small it does not mater. Just start one.

If at this point you are still debating whether or not you should believe that owning your own business is the key to wealth, then this book probably will do you no good. You truly need to understand and believe that, in order to become rich. And if you do not, there are hundreds of personal finance books that will basically tell you that very same thing in different ways. If you're not convinced, please read a few of them before you continue. What we are going to do is dive directly into what to do *after* you start your own business. Don't worry, if you have not started a business or have no idea what kind of business to start, I will cover some of that next.

There are two main categories in business that you can start. It can be a traditional business or a franchise where you borrow large sums of money from a financial institution or a willing relative. Or, it may be something small, for example a home-based business. This is where you keep your overhead and your start-up costs relatively low compared to a traditional business or franchise that may cost upwards in the hundreds of thousands of dollars or possibly millions of dollars to start. Keep in mind that numerous people starting a small business from inside their garages or on top of their kitchen tables have built them into huge multimillion and billion dollar companies. These are the types of businesses and the entrepreneurs that I will refer to within this book.

If you are interested in a traditional business and have the means of securing the capital or have a sense of where you are going to turn to secure capital, then start those steps now. Don't wait, begin today. As you do so this book can help immensely in reaching your final outcome. If you currently do not have a means to securing capital, which unfortunately most young people do not, then a small business may be perfect for you. Let's take a look at the options regarding a small business, possibly home-based.

A small business can mean that you want to start something new. In the example of Michael of Dell Computers, it can mean that you sell a product or service for another company. In the example of selling insurance, real estate, nutritional products, etc., you are following a prepackaged plan, which is very much like a franchise except that the set-up costs are much lower. There are programs sold for as little as a couple of hundred dollars to just a few thousand, where they outline the formula that someone has used to make money in the past. Examples of this type of business start-up kits are programs on buying and selling real estate, buying and selling cars, import/export businesses, or mail order often advertised on television or by the mail.

If your passion is to start something new but you don't know what, then please understand, whatever business you think of, know this, you can make a fortune at it. We live in a country where not just an invention, but even just a slight spin on an existing product or service can create millions. Examples of this are all around us and are too many to name. You have been exposed to so much information and opportunities around you thus far. Ideas are bubbling inside of you, or you can be inspired every time you turn on the television, or surf the Net. Even if you do not believe that you have an idea of what kind of business you would like to start today, I guarantee you do. You have an interest, hobby or something that drives you. Let's look at the example of the ex-professional snowboarder Andy Wolf (31), CEO of Premier Snowskate. When he realized that he could not snowboard forever, he did not just quit there and get a boring job, doing something he didn't like. He decided to take his love of the sport and grow it into his multimillion dollar business, with his own line of snowboard and skateboard hybrid, called The Snowskate. So take your love, or one of your passions, and turn that into a business this week.

If you absolutely have no idea of what to start, then maybe you can distribute for another company, or get involved in a prepackaged program that you purchased. I will discuss some of the most common type of prepackaged programs in Chapters 9 and 10.

So, you have an idea of what type of business you want to start. Great, you are going to begin that business this week. Maybe, you are not going to open for business and start selling this week, however you will begin the steps to eventually get there this week. Finally, you must now believe that as long as you intended to become rich you will always find a way to own a business. Even if your first or fifth business fails, you keep going on. Only when you ever decide that you never want to be rich, that is the moment that you can stop thinking about ever owning your own business. However, as long as you do want to become wealthy you'll firmly plant in your mind from this day forward, that the only way you can achieve this will be to own your own business.

I am not going to be able to hold your hand regarding owning your own business. You are going to have to do it, period. Now, we need to move on. We have a lot more important things to cover. You wanted to be rich, didn't you? You didn't want the sugarcoated solution to becoming rich, right? Well, then start this week. Okay, now let's move on to other things that you will need to do.

Your Daily Commitment

In order for you to become rich, you need to master and apply the proven success techniques for amassing wealth that are presented within this program. "How do I know this is what I need to do?" you may wonder. Simple. Follow this train of logic: If you are not rich today, then you are applying formulas (perhaps unconsciously) that are not geared toward making you rich. If you are making an *average* amount of money, then it follows that you are applying an *average* formula. My intention is to give you a *riches* formula that will lead you to *riches*.

But I must warn you. Do not be unrealistic and expect that after I give you the formula, you're going to become rich overnight. You are where you are today because you've been applying an average or perhaps even a *failure*-oriented philosophy every day and for a long time. To turn things around, once you have the *success*-oriented philosophy, you will need to practice that *every day* as well. If, for some reason, you cannot practice it everyday, you will need to commit to practicing it a minimum of three times a week—meaning that if you work a five day week, you need to practice at least three of those days. The information itself is not as important as it is for you to apply it as often as possible.

I'm telling you flat out, practicing this program once or twice will do absolutely nothing. This is because it is not a magic trick. It's a simple philosophy combined with a solid method for becoming rich that requires practice—just like becoming accomplished at any skill or any sport requires practice.

I have seen this program turn lives around, because it can open up incredible opportunities. But the only way that you can really *see* these opportunities is when the information you're about to receive in this program is second nature to you. At that point, the difference between an opportunity and a distraction will be very clear to you. But the average person, or to put it another way, the *untrained eye* will not be able to see it. However once this information is part of your subconscious, or part of your natural reactions, you will know a genuine opportunity when you see one. Whether you take it or not and how you deal with it will be up to you.

You will be training your mind, and your instincts, to see opportunities that others will miss—and that you too would have missed before you read and practiced these techniques. The simple reason most people are not able to get out of their current situation is because that they are not able to see opportunities. They are, in effect, blinded to opportunity. When they open a newspaper on Sunday, they do not see all the moneymaking opportunities that abound in that newspaper that cost them one dollar. They only see cars for sale, sports statistics, and what happened in the world yesterday. The only thing that registers as an "opportunity" is the fifty-cent discount coupons. But if you are able to absorb the philosophies that are presented in this book, you'll see much more than what I've presented to you. You will see opportunities way beyond this program. You'll see them in newspapers, books and magazines, in the media, whenever you meet somebody new. Wherever you look, you'll see possibilities for your success.

A Workout for Your Mind

As you may already know, to learn anything worthwhile usually takes practice. Whether you are trying to learn a sport, a subject in a class, a new language, or even how to do a new job, *practice* is essential. If you are trying to lose weight, it is very unrealistic for you to think that all you need to do is go to the gym for one week, work out really, really hard and you'll stay in shape for the rest of the year.

We can relate this program to a work out. Just as it takes sets of repetition to build muscles, it also takes repetition to build a new mindset. As I said earlier, if you are not rich right now, it's because you've been practicing techniques that do not lead to wealth. Staying with the gym analogy, if you've been lifting weights the wrong way, you will not show progress. But if you are shown the correct way—the efficient way—and you stick to the program and do not go back to your old ways, in time you will have the physique that you joined the gym intending to get.

Thus, consider the techniques within this program as a "workout for your mind." The technique is very simple. Basically I'm going to emphasize a few things that you need to do and a few things not to do. But the most important thing is that it is done *daily*. You know what the results are of falling off a diet. This is no different—except that sticking to my techniques will be—I assure you—much easier than sticking to a diet. And as you see the results, in the form of more money, your desire to stay the course will get stronger and stronger.

The Three Main Factors

There are just three main factors that you will need to be able to master, and begin applying in your life. I will explain them in detail later in this program. For now, I'm just going to give you an overview. This will give you a chance to get comfortable with them without trying to absorb too much at once. So for now, roll them around in your mind. Try them on for size. Play with them and see how they could fit. I have presented them to you in order of importance.

#1—Focus and Goals

Absolutely, without a doubt, this is the *number one* thing that you need to be able to master and apply. This factor is so crucial to attaining wealth that I am surprised to see that it is not taught in traditional schools. With the tools I will give you here, it will not matter what you want to be. The technique is not "How To Get Rich Doing Mail Order." Or, "How To Get Rich Doing Multilevel Marketing." It's how to get rich doing, reasonably of course, whatever you choose to do. This does not rule out those two professions. The point is, the technique is not limited to a specific career. Rather it is like a road map to succeeding in the career of your choosing.

#2—Time Management

I see a lot of people who are very confident and talented, yet are not able to get anything done. Months, even *years* later from the time that they had set a goal, they are no closer than the day they started. You probably know one or more of these people (you may even *be* one of these people). Almost everyone has a friend or relative who has said something like, "I am thinking about writing a book." Or, "I'm thinking about going into this business or that industry." And that's their problem—they're always *thinking* about it. But they never *take action* and *do* something about it. Instead, they've always got a million excuses why they *don't have time* to follow their dream. But this is not a lazy person. You will see that this person is extremely busy. But they are not doing the things that get them closer to what they *say* they really want to do. And one day, they sadly realize that life has passed them by.

#3—Delegation

While delegation is very important, it is something that you need not master immediately. It is further down the scale in priority level, which is why it is number three. But you will need to master it eventually. Focus on #1 and #2 in the beginning. (See how I'm trying to make this program as easy as possible for you?)

For now, just know this: delegation is important because there is just so much one person can accomplish in a day. And if you try to cheat on sleep to get more done, you may get away with it for awhile, but eventually it will wear you down and even effect your health. Many people are working extremely hard and do not know that there are techniques that can free up a lot of your time. At the same time, however, the technology that is available today, occasionally will pull time away from you, and can actually be counterproductive. But if you use the technology, combined with these formulas, they can help you leverage and understand how to best apply your time. You will be able to distinguish the difference between "working hard" and "working smart" and use it to your advantage. As you apply the techniques, you'll quickly realize if this or that choice is going to make you more or less efficient.

5 to 10 Times

So what do you need to do? You need to review this program AT LEAST 10 TIMES. I see you starting to hedge. "Ten times!" you're probably thinking right now, "you've got to be kidding!" But I'm not. Yes, at least 10 times. Possibly even more—it depends on your conditioning. If you had heard this information all your life, you'd probably only need to go over it two or three times. Because you are reading this information for the first time, it is not going to *sink in*—it is not going to become a part of your constitution. But after 5–10 times it *will* begin to sink in, to infuse itself in your very cells, so to speak. And in time it will be *yours*. You will own it. And it will be as if you always thought this way, for it will have pushed out, or superceded the thoughts that were bringing you average results.

Your parents, your school teachers, and others probably told you that there is a limited amount of opportunities in the world. They did not know that there is much more to the world than going to a 9-to-5 job and having your weekends off. They probably, unintentionally of course, filled your mind with messages about the limitations in the world. You may have been told that you're not good enough, or not to expect too much, or "life is hard, then you die." So to break through that heavy conditioning, you may need to review this material up to 10 times.

I have personally reviewed this material somewhere between 40 and 50 times. For me, it never gets old. The way I see it, every time I go through the program, I am getting consultation for *free*. I may have paid for it once when I first got it, but from then on it was one free session after another. Whenever I needed a little shot in the arm—a little booster—a pick me up—whenever I needed a little bit more counseling in a particular area of my life I would reread a certain portion of the program. And what amazes me is, each time I would find something new. Or I'd find I was seeing it differently—a way I hadn't thought of before. It was the same information, but I could see a new way to apply it to my life, or toward a certain obstacle that I was experiencing at that time. Somehow, hearing that *same* information again opened a *new* thought in my mind about to how to resolve it.

This is Nothing New

I do not claim to have discovered a *secret formula*. What I am telling you is something that has been around for centuries. It has been used to create success and wealth throughout time. It has been explained many different ways, but the information is basically the same. Truth is universal. It may have been interpreted many different ways, however the information itself is nothing new. Some people who have come up with the information (whether they were a personal development coach or a financial advisor) will say that they have "discovered the secret to wealth!" Sometimes they give the misconception that just by going through their four-hour or weekend course *one time*, the average person will immediately develop a new way to become rich, without putting forth any more effort. That is absolutely not true. Even though I generated a million dollars in business by age 26, I haven't lost my thirst for knowledge, nor my drive to improve. I am constantly growing and learning. Having a solid foundation is extremely important. Learn the basics, master them well and you can easily be well on your way to making a million dollars or more.

So how do you get this foundation? In one word: *repetition*. But I do not mean that you go through this book back-to-back 5 or 10 times in a row. You do need to take breaks in between. During these breaks, reflect on the world around you—read other books—take in other information. When you come back, the new info and the new experiences will give you a different outlook and raise your perspective to a whole new level. When you come back to this material fresh, energized and receptive, messages you weren't ready for in a previous read will then be revealed to you.

If I had lunch with somebody and presented all of my knowledge, meaning giving them hours and hours of personal consultation, and then I never saw that person again, I would guarantee you that person *will not* be able to apply even ten percent of the information I gave them. This is because people are not able to "absorb" in that way.

Just because you thoroughly went over this information once, it will do you no good. Even if you understand the English language perfectly and read every word carefully, this information will not become clear to you unless you can begin <u>applying</u> it to your life and begin <u>observing</u> the results. Then the information itself will take on an entirely new meaning. If you want this information to lead to amassing wealth, if you want this be one of your goals for life, then *right now* should be the tenth time that you've read this book. By then it will have become a part of your subconscious and thus will have become a part of your life. You'll begin to see opportunities that are not "visible" to other people. You'll begin to have opportunities arise that do not present for other people. That alone will put you so much more ahead of the game than most other people.

How Long Will It Take?

Often people who do not have a large amount of capital, or are not in a position where they can borrow enough money to start a traditional type of business, will start a home-based business. And there are countless home-based opportunities out there. But the first question I often hear people ask is, "How long will it take me to make money?" When they ask a question like that, I wonder if they are even committed to the project that they have started.

But I will entertain that question to make a point: "to the degree that you are able to commit is proportional to the time that you will see results." The quick answer to this question is that you will need to give any type of new project a minimum of one year. Even traditional businesses that have major financial backing rarely make money in their first year. This is not to say that they are necessarily losing money—usually they are at best breaking even. But it generally takes a minimum of one year to pay back the investment money, but two to three years is not unusual.

So one year is extremely conservative. I have seen people who begin a project—whether they sent away for something they saw on a TV infomercial, or they joined a multilevel marketing group—they try out the program for three to six months. Seeing that they are not making the kind of money that they had initially thought, they will quit. Because they still wish to be financially independent, they constantly look for another program and then another that will make them a considerable amount of money—and then give up within the same three to six months. Some of these people will even expect to make good money within *one* month. What these people end up doing is, in a period of a year, they may have tried two or three different programs and never made money in any of them. So they become a perpetual beginner—but never a *finisher*. They never see the great rewards of dedication and commitment.

So exactly how long will it take *you* to become rich? There is no pat answer because there are too many variables. For example, it will depend on the type of business that you choose. With today's technological advances such as the Internet, businesses can be connected throughout the world. You may reach the million dollar mark in two years, or five years, or it may take ten years. However, because you are now in the Information Age, and no longer in the Industrial Age, companies do not take generations to mature. Where in the past it would take 40 years to become established, that is no longer the case. However, there is a flip side to that. Many of the new generation, wanting to become entrepreneurs, see the high-speed of society and oftentimes interpret that to mean they can have immediate wealth. And they dream that this immediate wealth can be acquired putting forth very little effort.

Regardless of the marketing tactics that companies may use to get you to join, or purchase their program—regardless of the testimonials that they may have of people increasing their net worth or securing residual income within 1, 3 or 6 months, that should not be your timeline for determining whether the program will or will not work for you. It's all hype and it's not based in reality. I am telling you right up front that this is not a "get rich quick" program. Get rich quick programs get the *sellers* rich—the buyers only get poor faster. It is not my style to promise what I can't deliver. I'm telling you here and now it's going to take work and it's going to take time. But the rewards will be *real*, not "pie in the sky."

Empty Your Cup for Success

It doesn't matter what information you get, it's useless without one ingredient…ACTION! Real, honest, good information about how to make money (or whatever your field) from someone who has experience, is truly valuable. However, if you don't take ACTION and apply that information, it's useless. Plain and simple.

And here, once again, we discover that the "secret" lies inside of ourselves. Purchasing information about your subject, studying and learning all you can, is without a doubt a key to success. However, putting that information to use is the only way to *get that success!* Having a mentor, someone you can ask questions and bounce ideas off of is one of the best ways to get a leg up starting your own business. But be prepared to accept criticism to some of your ideas. You are, after all, just getting started and when you ask for the advice of one with more experience, honor that experience by at least accepting the information, and not arguing.

I remember a story about a very intelligent college professor who went to see a great Zen Master to learn all he could from the Master about the meaning of life. After traveling many miles to see the Master, they sat down together for tea. The professor began to go on at length about all he knew about Zen and what he thought was the meaning of life. The Master sat patiently listening and the few times he tried to speak, the professor quickly cut him off with his own feelings about whatever the Master had begun to speak of.

After a while, the Master asked the professor if he wanted some more tea. The professor said, "yes, thank you." As the Master filled his cup, he continued to pour the tea even as it ran over the top and onto the floor. The professor said, "What are you doing? The cup is full, stop pouring the tea!" As the Master stopped pouring he said, *"Just the same as the cup is full, so is your mind. You came here to gain more knowledge from me; however, all you have done is tell me everything you already know. Empty your cup so that you may learn from others."*

This concept seems very simple, just plain common sense, but it continues to amaze me how many people call me for advice and then argue with the information I share with them. While it is true that only you can build your business and change your life, but by using the guidance and information of others who are where you wish to be, you can certainly escape many pitfalls and mistakes and get where you want to be more quickly. But you must accept that information and guidance and then put it into practice.

Remember—empty your cup so you can learn and then take ACTION for success!

4

What Is This Big "Secret" To Wealth?

What's the Big "Secret?"

What is this great mystery that a lot of the wealthy people are hiding from the poor and the middle class? The secret is, there *is* no secret. Why is it so difficult to acquire wealth and why don't the rich share the knowledge? People are always looking for this big secret. Thinking that there is a magical formula that only the rich know. Thinking that the rich have a secret society that they do not allow the common people to participate in or learn from. Thus, the average person, whether they are poor or middle-class will often believe that since the rich are not telling them their secret that they now have an excuse to stay where they are. What is this big secret? What is the rich not telling us? How do I get in? If they only told me the secret I would be able to make a million dollars too!

Common Things I Hear Poor and Middle Class Say

There are some common misconceptions about wealthy people. Many people have negative ideas or stories about the wealthy. In fact some people strive to become wealthy so that they can have "their day." For them it's a power trip. They feel that one day when they become wealthy and are in a position where they have financial freedom, that they will be able to step on other people and treat them like dirt. They believe that once they become wealthy that they will not need to answer to anyone else. They will be *immune* to other people and will never again need to associate with the likes of those *poor slobs*. For example, there are many people who believe that once they build a home-based business, that will be their day of triumph. They look forward to the day when they can tell their boss to "take this job and shove it!" That will be their day of total bliss and from that day forward, they'll be able to mistreat or disgrace people at their leisure. *That* is an extremely poor and low class way of thinking. This sort of mentality toward your fellow man (and woman), regardless of your fine trappings, will definitely keep you in the low class you started in.

For people who think like this, what they will do is, as soon as they get any form of financial advantage over anybody else, they'll immediately "reward" themselves by treating others in a harsh or mean-spirited way—and they will start a chain reaction that they cannot stop in the future. They will have caused many people to despise them as an individual as well as a business person.

How the Rich Share the "Secret"

First of all, as I've stated before, there is no secret. That's because the information is all around us. You can go to a bookstore and there are literally hundreds of books on the subject of creating wealth. But people constantly talk themselves out of it. They say things like, "if it were that easy, *everyone* would be doing it." The reality is there is not *one way* to create wealth. Without being specific, there's a lot of workable programs out there, whether they are cassette tape sets, DVDs, video programs, workshops or books. And most of them work. The reason that they may or may not work all depends on you. Most of the people who buy these programs get extremely excited, they read or listen to the first chapter, then put the book down or turn the audiotape off. A little later, they get inspired again, maybe try the first assignment in the program. Then all of a sudden, they put the book back on their bookshelf and they forget about it. Or they'll say, "Maybe I'll go to Chapter Two tomorrow or next week." And of course, when that day comes, they get caught up in their life. They keep procrastinating. They push it back more and more. In the end, they never finish the course or book, let alone actually apply the information.

Do the rich share in the knowledge? Of course they do. Every time someone becomes a guru in business,articles are written about them. Magazine writers ask them questions and get clear and concise answers. They tell you how they did it. In fact, what I continually see is that when most of these entrepreneurs become wealthy, they are so excited that they cannot wait to tell the world how they did it. They are elated that they have reached a point where they are no longer struggling to cover their basic needs. They no longer have to worry about putting food on the table, dealing with creditors, or paying next month's rent. They are now in a position of *giving*. I see that these people want to inspire, pull other people up, and allow them to be able to do their best just like they did. They realize that there is *plenty* of room at the top and do not begrudge anyone else *their* success.

However, no matter how many times the rich share their information, be it on television giving interviews, in books or articles written about them, lecture tours, audiotapes, and countless other ways that they are trying to speak to you and share their secrets (methods) of success, certain people will continue to claim that the rich are special and want to keep it that way by hiding the "secret". Where do you stand? Are you someone who says you'll never be wealthy because the rich keep the trick to it a big secret? Or are you a person who says that the rich are trying to tell you something that you need to learn?

The Game of Pool

The game of pool is very well known. Most Americans have played it—especially during their college years. It is a common game that takes a great amount of skill and determination if you want to be real good at it. However, since it is easy to learn the basics, many people are able to have fun and play the first time, without looking too silly. In the game called billiards, you have a white ball (cue ball) that hits a solid or a striped ball (object ball), depending on your choice at the outset of a game. If you hit the cue ball straight, the colored ball goes straight. If you hit the cue ball slightly to the right, the colored ball goes at a slight angle to the left. And if you hit your cue ball to the left, the colored ball goes to the right. Simplified, the object of the game is do not sink someone else's balls into the pockets—only sink yours. Once all of your balls are in the pocket, sink the black 8-ball and you win. Obviously there is a more detailed explanation to the game. However, most college students can explain and demonstrate this game to a colleague in less than five minutes. And with a few hours of practice, a beginner can have a rudimentary game and give someone a certain amount of competition.

However, how long does it take for you to *master* this game? How many years of countless daily practice sessions on that green velvet table does it take for you to even be able to hit that ball totally straight, or exactly at a 45-degree angle? How long does it take to be able to "run the table," that is, to sink every shot without missing? For the average person, it may take several years.

You can apply this to just about any game—baseball, basketball, football. Think of any game or sport that you may be playing on a regular basis. Millions of people can *play* these games, but only a few hundred have *mastered* these games, and are rewarded accordingly with million dollar salaries. Take the game of chess. How long does it take for you to explain to someone how the pieces on a chessboard move? Five to ten minutes? But how long does it take for you to *master* the game of chess?

Thus, amateur versus professional sports serves as an analogy for the techniques that are presented in this program. There is no big secret to mastering the game of pool. It's simply a matter of learning the basics—that almost anyone can learn—then putting in the time and the practice until you become a pro. But many people are looking for this big magical "secret" that they believe is unachievable except by a select few. They are looking for something that is so astonishing that when they hear it for the first time, or see it for the first time, they will be inspired to a point that they now want to learn this brand-new task, this amazing skill that almost no one else knows. And then they will become enlightened.

However, this is not how it works. How it works has nothing to do with anything magical or spiritual or something that is so secretive that only you will know. The reality is, the actual information itself has nothing to do with how to play the game. It's very basic information, and your success is all going to depend on your commitment to taking that simple information and choosing to apply it, without quitting midstream.

To give you an example, did you know that if you were able to hit the cue ball and your object ball perfectly straight or at a precise angle of your choosing, you would be able to defeat 95% of the pool players that you may encounter at any local bar, college student union, or upscale sports bar? And win without being able to do those fancy bank shots, combinations, or trick shots. However, most people will not take the time or expend the effort to learn the fundamentals. So I ask you, are you prepared to apply the basic information that you will have learned?

Because the information that will be provided in this program will show you what are the simple techniques that you need to be able to master in order for you to acquire wealth. It will not show you how to do fancy bank or trick shots that may impress someone on the occasion that you will be able to hit it just right. Rather, this program is designed to show you how to hit the ball straight or slightly at a 45-degree or 25-degree angle that will basically allow you to beat most players. You do not need to be able to do these fancy or advanced techniques. Just get these simple basics down, and you're in.

What are you trying to accomplish? Are you a trying to accumulate a vast amount of information that is not applicable in the real world? Or are you trying to accomplish the end result? To be able to be financially free? You need to ask yourself this. If you are trying to attain a vast knowledge of information that is fascinating and is something that you can philosophize with other colleagues, but is not applicable, then this is not for you. The information in this program is extremely simple. In effect, I will show you how to "hit the cue ball straight so your colored ball will go straight." And I will show you how to "hit the ball slightly to the right or left, so your ball will go slightly to the left or right." And in this program I will explain that you need to *practice*.

Martial Art Example

Finally, I can show you something you can use in your daily life. Many people aspire to one day becoming financially free or wealthy. They want to have their dream home, or that beautiful house on the beach. At the same time, most people have the basic need to feel safe. I can show you a martial art move to protect or defend yourself in most hostile situations.

Some of you may never have the fear of walking down any street in your town. However, many people who are living in a metropolitan city in this country do not have that same sense of security. Some of us actually need to think ahead when we go out the door, or get in or out of our cars, or wherever we need to feel a little safer. Some people may feel they need to be able to defend themselves in any situation.

If you are in physical danger, regardless of the size of your attacker, what do you think is the one move that you can do that will immobilize your attacker? I am sure that many of you already know the answer to this question. You may have seen it demonstrated in a public service spot on TV, or you may have seen it in the movies. But if you do not already know how, in one move, to completely immobilize an attacker coming at you who is twice or three times your size and strength, what do you think that move is?

Think of all the martial art training or self-defense schools and programs out there. I have known many students who go to these schools. The first day, they are bubbling with enthusiasm because of something that they may have seen in the media. They've come to learn how to be a martial artist. They want to be able to look and move like a martial artist that they have seen in the movies or on television. They ask the teacher or master to teach them something today. The master may teach them something like a simple defensive move. The students practice that lesson and then return the following day, eager to move on to something new in their desire to become closer to attaining a black belt. But the master shows the students the same punch or the same defense. Some students will say, "Master, please show me something new—something fancy." But the wise master says, "You need to learn these basic techniques." Over a period of several months, the master may show his students a small series of moves. To give you an example, Tae Kwon Do has under 10 basic punches and kicks that you need to be able to master in order for you to become a black belt. Just being able to master those ten techniques provides you with enough skill to be able to defend yourself in most situations. Some students may take the class for two to six months and complain that the master is still showing them the same techniques over and over. They get bored, say they've had enough, and quit. Unfortunately, some of you will do the same with this program—become annoyed with the simplicity of it and quit.

But back to my earlier statement. This is the one simple move that you can use to immobilize anyone. You don't need to learn ten. And even though I cannot see you, I will be able to teach it to you. It is very simple: when an attacker comes at you with or without a weapon, simply drop down to his waist level (I'm saying *his* because unfortunately most attackers are male). Take your strongest hand and quickly grab upwards to his crotch as hard as you can, and squeeze until the attacker drops. That is it. You just learned how to immobilize an attacker in most situations. Obviously, if the attacker is armed with an AK-47 and is wearing a sports cup, this technique will not work.

The point is, this technique is something that most people already know how to do. There is no secret. However, when it is executed perfectly, it almost seems like magic. It almost seems like a big secret. And obviously you now know that it is not. This technique is something that will take less than 30 seconds to learn. However, it may take years for you to be able to master it so that it works *every* time in *all* situations. And the reason is, it takes *practice* to be able to condition your mind to where you can overcome the fear of improperly executing this technique, and gain maximum confidence instead.

Hopefully, you'll never need to use this technique in a real-life situation. Even though this technique is extremely simple to use, in an actual situation most people will forget how to use it. They will freeze up and not be able to execute it. And this is what I see in the world when it comes to being able to manage your own personal finances. I have seen that although most people know that you can utilize a simple technique to accumulate wealth, and it does not take some secret method, still they are afraid to execute it. They choose not to learn or practice it just in case they ever need to.

What will *you* do? What will your choice be—inaction? Or will you choose to practice over and over the simple techniques that can lead you to riches?

5

Focus And Goals & The 4 Keys to Success

Welcome to a World Where Your Future is in Your Own Hands

That is of course where it has always been. In the past, however, you may have thought your hands were tied behind your back! No more. The program you hold contains a powerful message that tells how you can do something with your life and how you can fulfill your dreams. It is not the only plan of attack you can use to change your life. There are countless others. Many people just aren't suited to handle most of them.

This plan does not require that you hold a degree in upper level management for it to work it successfully. It *does* require you hold a degree in something called "Common Sense." That's right, good, hard, and effectively applied common sense. But don't get me wrong, it will not be the easiest thing you have ever done, either. It requires a high degree of professionalism. That is, a professional attitude toward your endeavor. While I earlier used the analogy of a game, in practice, this is *not* a game, it's a serious undertaking.

The bottom line is very plain. Unless *you* do it, it's never going to get done. It takes a lot more than a great idea to put a dollar in your pocket. This book and all the rest are worthless unless the reader decides to expend the effort to actually follow through. And not half-heartedly, either. Too many people in this world perform way below their potential. And that's really too bad. But that's just the way some people are. Millions of people every year at least try to do something about their position in life. And now it's up to you to do more than just try. It's up to you to make it work.

Focus and Goals

Maintaining focus and having distinct, realistic goals is the first step to attaining wealth. Almost every personal development coach will tell you this. Not everyone says it the same way, but the truth is the same—there might be a slightly different interpretation from one coach to another, but it all boils down to this: there are *three keys* to success. *First*, determine where you are now, and where you want to go. *Second*, determine how you are going to get there, then take action and follow though. *Third*, is remember to evaluate whether or not what you are doing is working, and if not, adjust.

It is very important that you determine your goals and why you want them. Otherwise, it is like starting out on a long journey without a map. This tactic could have you going around in circles indefinitely. You also need to know how much money you want to make, and what position do you eventually want to be at in life.

Next is to determine a plan on how to get there—whether you are going to follow a mentor, or study other successful people and create a plan. Whatever it is that you study, the next important thing is to take action and follow through. In this section there are techniques on how to prevent procrastination, which is the enemy of taking action. Most people will have high dreams and goals, will have all this untapped potential, yet will never actually take action nor follow through. This is the killer in life.

I see this in a lot of multilevel companies where people get into the program, try it for two to three months, then lose interest and quit. They do not realize that they need to invest, on average, a minimum of a year to actually *begin* to make a decent amount of money, or get a decent response from their efforts. Most likely there will be a point in time where you start to have doubts, or start to second guess yourself, or start to get weary. This is where it is crucial to keep your focus, stay the course and follow through on your game plan. When you do, it's like when a runner gets their "second wind." Suddenly, when you think you don't have anything left, you get this invigorating burst of energy.

Last, you need to be able to evaluate and adjust. However, some people want to evaluate and adjust after only a couple of months—whether it is real estate, or an investment program, or whatever. The time to evaluate and adjust is a fine line that's often hard to determine. However it's extremely important to know where that fine line is. You need to trust that as you get better and better, your instincts will kick in and you'll just *know* when it's time to take a different action, or whether you should stick with the formula you're on.

There are people who will say that the key to success is simply positive think-ing—and leave it at that. Don't get me wrong, positive thinking has its place, but it can sometimes do you wrong. For example, when we say to ourselves, "nothing is wrong, nothing is wrong" when all is crashing down around you. I encourage people to be realistic—to see what is going on—to stay out of denial—and when it becomes crystal clear to you that you're in need of shifting (evaluating and adjusting), then take those steps.

I love to speak to student groups such as the FBLA (Future Business Leaders of America) at various high schools. When students ask me, "What is the thing that I should do that will give me the best chance of success like you have reached?" I say, "Join a multilevel group." Why? You'll get an education that you cannot get at any college or high school. You'll learn firsthand how to be able to "think outside the box." For example, there is only a one percent chance that you will be wealthy by the time you are 65. Schools just don't say that to the students, thinking that this is going to discourage them. They do not realize that shading them from the truth is not benefiting them either. It is sad to see it when some of these people grow up and realize that for the first time after they've reached the age of 40. With network marketing companies you will learn the important skill of *networking*. To be able to walk up to someone and say, for example, "Hello, my name is Ken. This is what I do, what do you do? Perhaps we can help each other?" And that is very important. I used to be an entertainer. I performed in front of tens of thousands of people. However, I was not able to walk up to some-one and say, "this is what I do," until I joined a network marketing company.

I see people who know what they want, take action, and follow through, but they stay with a company for three to five years and they do not make enough money. They got what they got from it, to think outside the box, learned how to network and come out of their shell. However, they are locked into the "faith mentality." They think that come hell or high water, this company is going to make them all the money in the world. This is blind faith—almost like a religion where they think they have to suffer for their dream. That is where the danger comes in. That is where you need to be able to evaluate and adjust. And that is where it becomes extremely important to ask yourself, "I got what I want, is it now time for me to move on? Is it time for me to change my program? Did I learn all I can learn?" If the answer you get is "yes" then great! It's time for you to move on.

Using Pleasure and Pain to Your Advantage

Believe me, I'm not a masochist, but one thing that I like to do is use *pain* as a way to motivate me. Focusing on the pleasurable end result of what you wish to achieve is important. But you'll do more things to try to avoid something that will cause you pain. Even a poor student will cram or at least open the book before a big test. This is because the fear or pain of knowing absolutely nothing on the test motivates even the poor student to review the chapters. But the pleasure of doing well was not enough to motivate them to study throughout the semester.

Let's use an example that has to do with money. Two scenarios: First, let's say there is a school promotion. If you get an 85% or higher on a test you'll be given $1,000. How hard would you study? Second scenario: Let's say you made a bet with someone. If you *do not* get a test score that is 85% or higher, $1,000 will be deducted from your savings account. They have your account number and your authorization. And if you do not have $1,000 at the time the test scores come back, and you lose, you will owe $1,000 and it will appear on your credit history. Which one would you study harder for?

The human mind will do more things to avoid painful situations than it will do to get pleasure. I subscribe to the the DuPont Registry. In the magazine, they have listings of exotic islands or mansions for sale. They also have exotic cars, yachts and airplanes. I go through it to look for "toys." Recently, I was looking for a Lamborghini. And if I were to one day own a Lamborghini that would certainly give me pleasure. But it doesn't really motivate me to work harder, to put in the necessary extra hours.

However, this is what I do. Whenever I go to the grocery store, to the mall, or Home Depot, I may encounter a store employee who is my age. They may even be somebody who I went to high school with. I do not have a college degree. I finished high school and took some college classes. I assume that the person working behind the counter, or loading up the boxes, probably finish high school and maybe took a class here or there in college. The *pain* that I've used, and I continually use today, is I imagine that I could have that person's job. That I could be getting paid what that person gets paid. Our educational level was identical, and we roughly grew up in the same neighborhood, yet, as I stand there staring at this person, I remind myself that I make more money in one hour than that person is making the entire day. This person will load boxes day in and day out, and I will make more money in one week than this guy will make in an entire year.

But if I do not continually train myself and practice the techniques presented in this program—if I do not make it a priority to make the techniques in this program a daily ritual, I may end up having a job similar to this person. I have used this type of motivational technique for years. I would also see people five years older than me who had a lifestyle that would horrify me. I kept saying to myself, "If I don't practice these techniques *that* will be my life."

So one of the things that I did was, I heard that my distant Aunt by marriage was a "Diamond" in Amway. "Diamond" is one of the top positions you can reach in this multilevel marketing company. As soon as I found out that I had a relative in Amway I sought her out. I asked to join the Amway organization under her. Back then, I remember seeing a couple of things that disturbed me. I remember seeing people who were 10, 20, 30 years older than me who were realizing for the first time in their life that in this country you rarely become financially free by working for someone else. Most of these people were working very hard, had lots of bills and responsibilities, and discovered that they were not getting any further in life, or that retirement was going to be extremely difficult or impossible. And I thought at that time, "Wow, what an age to finally come to that realization!"

I did not want to experience *that* reality when I became older. So I repeatedly told myself that if I do not practice the techniques, I'll end up like the people in this room. The other reason why I kept attending Amway meetings was because I always liked what the speakers had to say. Back then I did not know that there were books and audio programs that presented simple ways to set goals and plan your future. I liked the fact that these Amway meetings had a speaker who was always saying to the audience, "Where are you going to be five years from now?" And I was scared whenever I heard the question—but being scared is sometimes good. If you do not get scared yourself, you could end up like all the people who got *downsized* in the past couple years. You could end up like some of your parents, or your aunts and uncles who have lost their jobs and are scrambling for new jobs—some even for *entry-level* at their age. So if you want *real* motivation—don't conger up a picture of your dream house in your mind—just look at some person around you who has a job or a life that horrifies you.

If you have a job right now, but do not like what they pay you, or do not like your job, period, can you imagine if you're still at that same position in life five years from now? Can you imagine you are getting paid the same for your same job five years from now, and it just gets worse when the company tells you that you are going to be laid off. You go looking for another job, interview after interview, and no one wants to hire you.

This is an interactive exercise that I suggest you do daily—especially if you're having trouble getting started. Whenever you go out, observe people on the street, at the store, your friends, your acquaintances and even your family members who are struggling to make ends meet. If you *give* yourself the pain (imagine it and try to feel it) you will do more things to avoid it. If you give yourself the pain of seeing these people, their lifestyle, their financial situation and envision—that is, *picture* yourself ending up just like them, or that you end up staying the way you currently are, this should hopefully jolt you or jumpstart you into moving toward your goal.

Some personal development programs have exercises where you write down what will happen if you do not apply yourself daily. These are excellent exercises. And I encourage you to do them to enhance your daily interactive exercises. For some people, writing it, and seeing it on paper is more powerful than seeing it in their mind's eye. Also, some people just may not be able to do visualization exercises, because it is outside their comfort zone. In brief, what you do is, on a piece of paper write for 5 minutes and describe in detail, without ever letting your pen stop, what kind of life you will have 3 years from now—if you keep doing what you have been doing. Detail meaning, what kind of professional and personal life you will have, where you live, do you own a home, what kind of car you own, how many vacations you can take in a year, etc. You will describe all of that in detail. Once you are finished, now you can read your future. That should scare the heck out of you. Now you know you need to change and apply these techniques daily.

I have tried the writing exercises in the past. They are an excellent strategy. And, I see so many people that I do not want to be all around me all the time that I have no problem using them as away to put pain on myself—the person that you do not want to become is often living and breathing and talking right around you. I do both visualization *and* writing. Others of you will prefer writing only because you have what you don't want right on paper in front of you, and you do not need to visualize or imagine who you don't want to become. Finally, just be sure you *also* write down the steps you are going to take to prevent this from happening to you. Otherwise it can spiral you down into depression.

Remember, the sky is the limit. You can be young and be rich. Although, as I said, people will do more to avoid pain, it is important for positive encouragement to also see what is possible. A very real tool that I love to look at every now and again is Forbes' ranking of the Top 40 Under 40 Richest Individuals in the world. This information can be obtained on their website. I skip all the ones that have inherited their money and immediately read the ones who made their fortune by starting a business. Forbes tells their age, how much they are currently worth, and usually the story of how they accumulated their wealth. For me, that is the exciting part. Even if their story is not on Forbes.com's website they will often refer you to the entrepreneur's website and you can look it up under the 'History' of the company. To follow is an example of a typical success story that you can see on the Net. Make sure to constantly read stories and examples of how big you can get.

The Possibilities

I do not like to advocate Dot-coms or Internet companies as a means to attaining wealth because we still do not know what is going to be their final outcome. However, we cannot ignore some of the success stories we have seen that have sustained through the bust of the Internet bubble. That said, Jerry Yang (33), and David Filo (36) started Yahoo while they were students at Stanford. They set out to find a way to make sense of the chaotic Internet. In doing so, they created a searching program that pulls information based on what subject you type in—now known as a "search engine." Having started in their early 20s, they are to date two of the richest "under 40 entrepreneurs" according to Forbes magazine. Their net worth is somewhere in the neighborhood of $500 million.

They set the stage for the people who came after them—such as Sergey Brin (29) and Larry Page (27) who developed Google.com. Even with all the search engines available by the time they came into the market, they saw that whenever you typed in a subject to search, such as "College Tuition," you would get anything from college courses to a thesis that an undergraduate wrote about how financial aid helped her develop the responsibility of paying her own tuition. Add to that, "how the new bronze tone makeup line is making the freshmen women look like oranges with hair," plus renegade angry articles regarding the rise of power of the *devil* who increased the college tuition in this country—and a small bank in a town in Wisconsin that offers tax benefits if your loan were applied to your child's school tuition. You got all this bologna when all you wanted to know was, "How much do students pay for tuition at different universities around my local area?" Before Google.com, whenever you searched for *any* subject you would get countless websites that did not pertain to that topic, or you would get millions of websites and would not know where to begin. Sergey and Larry developed a way to selectively narrow your search.

Google.com currently generates around $70 million in annual sales by selling advertisement. All this based on ideas and the application of information. What is it that we can learn from this? What is it that they know that we need to begin to understand for us to make it in the new millennium? As they say on TV, "stay tuned…"

6

How to Achieve True Success in Life

Let's do a quick exercise. I don't want you to simply read this program and not *apply* something that will help shape your future. I would like to at least give you one exercise so that you will begin to understand how powerful it can be when you simply write things down. I want your hopes and desires no longer to be a dream that you may have as you doze off to sleep, and when morning comes, you are absolutely no closer to realizing your goals. This exercise, although a very simple one, will begin the process of solidifying most of your financial dreams.

If you like this type of exercise, there are many programs by various personnal development coaches, such as Tony Robbins, that will drill down and really help you get to the essence of your goals. They'll also assist you in mapping out a strategy to attain them. If this is of interest to you, use an Internet search engine to get you to Tony Robbin's (or whichever personal coach you prefer) website. If you choose Robbins, I would suggest you get his *Personal Power 2* program. It costs a couple hundred dollars and is well worth it. Think how much your college classes cost you or your parents. For a couple hundred dollars you can shape your life and really map out who you are going to become, having your wishful thinking disappear and having goals of creating riches start appearing as a reality in your life.

Are you ready to begin the exercise? Start by getting a regular letter-size blank piece of paper and a pen. Or you can use the example from the next page and make a copy of it. Write down 3 to 5 goals you have for this year. These may have been your New Year's resolutions—even if it is currently November. Whatever they are—resolutions or dreams that you have had—that you would like to accomplish by one year from today. Please write each goal underneath one another in a bullet-like format.

Focus & Goals

This Year's Goals

Income Goals (Annual)

_____

Year One

_____

Year Two

_____

Year Three

_____   _____

Sign   Date

Year Five Material Goals

_____

_____

_____

_____

_____

_____

_____

_____

_____

_____

_____   _____
Sign   Date

These goals can be anything that's important to you such as "stop smoking," or "lose twenty pounds," or "take a cross-country trip." But be sure to include at least one or two business or financial aspirations that you have. For example, you may have heard that people can make a lot of money in real estate. So you would write something like, "this year I would like to work at a real estate company." Or, "I would like to purchase my first real estate investment with no money down." Take a few minutes right now and write down those three to five goals that you would like to accomplish in one year.

When you've finished, right below that I want you to write "one year." To the right of that, please write down the amount of money that you wish to be making one year from today. Be realistic, but at the same time, be bold. Put down an amount that will be a stretch for you—but not entirely out of your reach.

Now, below that, please write "three years." To the right of that, write down how much money you wish to be making annually three years from today. Now you can reach further—perhaps triple the yearly amount you wrote for one year—maybe more? Again, try to be honest with yourself, but at the same time, be generous. If you learn and practice the techniques daily, by this time you could be increasing your income exponentially.

And now, below that please write "five years," and to the right of that, write down how much you wish to be making annually five years from now. If you are the type who is able to commit and follow through, there is no way this five year figure should be conservative. So let your imagination run wild.

Okay, we're not done yet. Below your five year figure write down "Year Three-Five Material Goals." If there is not enough room use a second sheet. We live in a materialist society, and this technique works—especially if you are able to visualize not only how much money you would like to be making, but also what it will get you. So write down 5–10 things that you intend to have in your life three to five years from now. It may be a place of your own, or a car. But do not just write down "a car." Be specific! Write down what type of car. Is it a BMW or a Cadillac? Also, would you like to be married or have children? Most young people will say they cannot get married right now because they would not be able to support a family. But with commitment to this program, that is all going to change. Would you like to own a house? If so, what kind of a house? How many bedrooms and which neighborhood? How about owning your own company?

Once you have written down your 5–10 cherished possessions that you *will* have in 3 to 5 years, there is one thing left to do. At the very bottom of this piece of paper, draw a line and boldly sign the document. The reason for this is because there's a little more *weight* to these pieces of papers that you have signed and committed to, and that you'll be constantly moving toward. You see, this is not merely a piece of scratch paper. It's a *contract* between you and the universe.

Now comes the most challenging part of this exercise. What you need to do at this point is to take that piece of paper and a piece of Scotch tape, and *tape it to the wall in your bathroom*—right beside your mirror. The reason that I am saying to put it up on your bathroom wall is because I am assuming that room is the first room that you see in the morning. It is a room that you need to go into when you wake up and brush your teeth and comb your hair. If you place it in an out-of-the-way spot in your kitchen, or on the back side of your closet door, it can easily be missed or dismissed. You may skip breakfast, or on your closet door, clothes may cover it. Whatever you do, never put this goal sheet inside a folder. You will never see it again.

You need to be reminded daily of your one year goals, and your three to five year goals. You need to be daily reminded of the data you signed for on this piece of paper, so as the weeks and months go by, you are continually aware that you are moving toward it—or away from it if you start slacking off. Every morning, as you see this piece of paper stuck up next to your mirror and you get reminded of your goals, as your day begins, you'll be reminding yourself if you have done anything yesterday to get you closer to anything on that piece of paper with your signature on it.

I complete this exercise or a version of it at least three times a year. Over time, goals in life change. As these changes are re-documented, my aspirations in life become clearer.

Your bathroom may be shared with another person, which may open up your goal sheet to ridicule. But if you are prepared to show people where you want to go, it makes your commitment to your goals more powerful. It brings you up to the point where you like telling people that "this is where I am prepared to go." And it helps solidify your resolve that there's no turning back.

Actually it is more effective if other people can see it. However you can do whatever accommodates your comfort level. If you do not want to have your goals shared with other people, then the bathroom is not a place where you can post it. In that case, find another place to put this piece of paper that is a location you'll see every day. Remember do not place this piece of paper in a folder, unless it is a folder that you have to open daily. If it is a folder that you do not open daily, the effectiveness is completely lost. Five years from now, you'll be cleaning your room or you'll be throwing stuff away and you'll come across your goal sheet that never did anything for you and became a lost dream.

How the Physical, Emotional, Spiritual and Financial all Interlock

This program is designed primarily for young people who are trying to step up from the poor and middle class. You will be given the hard facts and techniques that you need to apply *every single day* for you to get the maximum results within the shortest amount of time. And although this program is centered on mastering the financial aspects of your life, I do need to let you know about the other factors of life that will affect your financial goals.

The first is the *emotional* factor—how you feel about yourself and/or how you feel about your relationships. The *physical* factor is your health. And the *spiritual* factor is how you may feel connected to a Greater Cause than yourself. For some, this will mean how you feel your relationship is with God, or the Higher Spirit. It may involve a way that you'll give back to the community, such as though charity work.

While I do feel these are all important, and all contribute to having financial success, I am not going to go into a lot of detail with them. The reason being, each aspect alone is an entire program within itself. And there are already other exceptional books available that cover each of these subjects. However, I cannot neglect their importance.

I am sure that most people do not want to grow up to become like Ebenezer Scrooge. No one wants to become an old, decrepit man, with very poor health, living in a huge mansion by yourself, and harassed by your own demons, just to be able to claim the title of "wealthiest man in town." If you concentrate *only* on the financial and let the other aspects, of your life deteriorate, you will likely be unbalanced—and unhappy. The disparity will actually drag down other parts of your life. All four aspects emotional, physical, spiritual and financial are like four pillars holding you up. If one or two are falling, even though one is a very strong, it's unlikely you'll excel to your full potential.

You could be amassing a huge amount of wealth. Yet you are smoking 2 to 3 packs a day, eating an extremely poor diet of junk food, and drinking or taking drugs regularly. It's only a matter of time until your health will deteriorate—at first slow—then as the accumulative effects pile up, the decaying process will accelerate. Let's say you were destined to live into your 70s or 80s. Due to the aforementioned accumulative effects, your life could be cut short and you find that at age 40 you have a terminal disease. Thus, you just cut your full potential in half. So what you have set out to do at the very beginning is undermined because of your determination to only excel in one of the four.

We can see this example in some of the Rock Stars or the Movie Stars who become successful very quickly. They do not know what to do with all their money. They begin a wild course of abusive behavior and eventually their health fails. They no longer can adequately use their mind for their creativity, and their career goes down the drain. I am deeply saddened to say that another example is my mother. Although she did not use drugs, health was not something that was a priority with her. Even though she had a great relationship with her children, and had a successful career, various bad habits eventually caught up to her and she had passed away with cancer before she hit 40.

Okay, let's say you are doing well financially, you're experiencing tip-top physical health, but you are not able to control your own emotions. You frequently lose your temper or go through deep depressions, or you're not able to maintain healthy relationships that make you feel good on a daily basis. Any of that is going to have repercussions in your physical health with the amount of stress that it will cause you. It will start to seep into the financial aspect of your life. Then as you try to concentrate on what is going to make you financially independent, your focus will constantly be diverted. Soon, every business decision that you need to make will have major stress attached to it.

In regards to your spirituality, I am not here to force any religion or belief onto you. However, people have a human need to contribute or to feel a connection with your Maker, Greater Spirit or something greater than oneself. The connection to 'something greater' can also be a *cause* where you are volunteering, helping others to move toward your vision of a better society, or to participate in a big brother or sister program in your area to give a child someone to look up to. Thus, your spirituality does not necessary need to be a participation in a religion. When you are successful in all the other aspects of your life, but you have been neglecting your spiritual need to contribute, demons will come to attack you when things go bad. Yes, demons. Not the mythological or biblilogical demons, but the demons from your own mind that will infest your psyche with self-doubt and a feeling of "no one else cares about me anyway." When, 'things go bad' meaning the absolute and the unavoidable Ups and Downs that you will surely experience throughout this financial journey, without the spiritual connection it is extremely easy for someone to immediately become abusive toward themselves. Which again will begin to drain the potential of your finances.

If you are aware of any shortcomings in the physical, emotional, or spiritual aspects of your life, I strongly suggest that you get books or tapes by other coaches that can help you. I realize, in choosing this course, the financial factor is probably something that you want to spearhead in your life. And it is perfectly okay that currently you want to work on increasing your net worth. All four pillars do not need to be *equally* important to you. Just be aware that they *all* are important to varying degrees. You may be in top physical shape, have a great relationship with a significant other, and regularly go to church (or use a daily meditation technique)—thus you do not need to work on the other pillars of your life. And the reason that you got this program was to increase the financial pillar. That is great. I just feel that balancing the four pillars is such an important detail that I see a lot of people overlook and I did not want you to fall into the same trap.

Utilizing a Previous Technique

Another thing that you may wish to do is a variation on the interactive exercise that was presented earlier. If you remember, I discussed using the reminder of people around you that you do not want to become to motivate you—looking at their position and saying, "absolutely not for me!"

If you are the type who does not like to dwell in any kind of negative, here is a similar method for you: *reverse* the technique and focus on the lifestyle or personage of someone who you admire—or what you would like to *become*. However this interactive exercise has *two* steps. With the previous technique there are plenty of people around you who demonstrate where you do not want to go. So it is easy to visualize yourself as becoming one of them if you do not apply yourself. *This* interactive exercise will require that you also begin to *network* with successful people. As you meet or surround yourself with people who have reached their financial goals you are now in a position where you can more effectively visualize yourself *becoming* like them if you apply the techniques in this program. The other thing that you will be able to do, obviously, is *ask* them what was important to them in accomplishing their current wealth.

Entrepreneur Story

You have probably seen those television commercials for the video series *Girls Gone Wild*. You may not agree with the material that is presented on the video or DVD series. However, the entrepreneurship of 29-year-old, **Joe Francis**, is an example of how using his focus and goals, plus innovation and creativity built his company. Francis did not invent anything. Looking back at what was popular on television, you can easily see that there was nothing new about the concept. For years we have seen Jerry Springer take his show to a Spring Break in Mexico. Then there is the *Wild On* series on E! Television that visits popular teen vacation spots. Joe just used a variation of what the public was already wanting and combined it with great marketing.

If you're not familiar with the GGW series, a cameraman goes into nightclubs, Mardi Gras, and Spring Break parties where young women are coaxed into peeling off their tops. Advertised as "Raw! Real! and Uncut!" the girls look like people that you may know, or the girl next door. They're obviously not supermodels or porn stars. With the influence of alcohol and party revelry, they end up flashing themselves for some flattery and a free shirt. Last year, Joe's company sold 4.5 million videos and DVDs for up to $19.99 a piece. If you calculate that out, it's an annual sales of up to $90 million a year.

How did it all start? In 1997, Joe was working as the production assistant on the syndicated show, *Real TV*. It showed bloopers, gaffes, and other unusual home videos submitted by viewers. Joe noticed that a lot of the videos that the viewers were submitting were either too violent, or too risqué for television—and he saw an opportunity. He knew that people would want to see some of these outrageous videos. He always wanted to be a business owner and liked the idea of being a direct marketer. There's no middleman, and no storefront. You sell directly to the consumer via mail. He used his credit cards to license a few of the videos. He spliced the footage together and marketed them under the title, *Banned From Television*. It showed shocking clips such as actual car crashes, and even a woman getting hit by a train. It did $10 million in sales in one year. Knowing how to adapt to America's changing tastes, he eventually moved on to *Girls Gone Wild*.

7

Time Management

Through my experience with several marketing companies, I have seen extremely talented people with so much potential, but who were unable to get anywhere financially. And for a long time I wondered what was it that they were lacking that successful people had. Some of these people actually had the *focus and goals* portion of mapping their future written down. They had actually gone through all the exercises that their coaches had set. They may have done the *goals-taped-in-bathroom* technique. They were always busy, always running around, and yet they never got anything accomplished. I then realized they were the proverbial "chickens with their heads cut off."

The reason that they were not able to accomplish their goals or to be able to move out of their static situation, was that they had not mastered the second essential technique, *time management.* Without this simple step, no matter how many goals, dreams or aspirations that you may have, and regardless of talent, creativity, or how smart you are, you will never get anything done. People's aspirations and potentials can be easily realized if they simply apply time management to their lives. Regardless of evolution and how far the human race has come, we still have limitations within our minds. The sooner you are able to realize this, the quicker and easier it will be to make the transition and master this technique.

There is a myth that is preventing many people from reaching their goals. The technological revolution has provided us with many conveniences such as the Internet, cell phones, faxes, e-mail, instant messaging, Web browsing, and the like. The myth is that all of these conveniences always make mankind more productive by freeing up more time. In fact, these technological advances make us believe that we have gone to the next level of intelligence. In actuality, many of these technological advancements have *slowed* the human brain to a level of luxurious relaxation. Many of these devices do our thinking for us. Thus we actually become more lax—more lazy—rather than more productive. And for some of us, we spend more time *learning* how to use them than we do actually using them.

The technological revolution has allowed individuals and companies to continually employ newer and newer products every year in order to communicate with each other as well as to save time. At the beginning of the last century, the way that people communicated with each other was either by mail or a telegram. At the beginning of this century, if you take a random group of 100 people and observed how they communicate with the world on a weekly basis, the methods are overwhelming. We are not talking about some obscure technology that just came out last week or at the latest Computer Expo, but how many of us Americans are communicating every week.

Let's list some of them: home phone, work phone, cell phone, voicemail, answering machine or service, personal Web sites, e-mail, attachments or downloading and uploading files, E Cards, instant messaging, faxes, memos, snail mail, FedEx and messengering. And to help organize and schedule everything for the devices that we use we have, Palm Pilots, internet-connected cell phone, desktop, and laptop. And there is an endless amount of software that people use to either create documents, spreadsheets, presentations, and an unending amount of software used to transfer this information.

If you think of all the ways that we communicate, this was all designed initially to save time and add convenience. Let me ask you a couple of questions, "How has it worked for you lately?" And, "Do you find you have all this *free time* each day as a result?" My point is that all of these technological advances can actually eat up the free time you would have had if you'd only heeded the old K.I.S.S. adage, *Keep It Simple Stupid!*

My advice is know that the technology exists, understand how it is used, but immediately determine whether this new device or communication method is just the hottest new thing, or the cutest little toy—or is it going to get you to your end goal. Unless communication is your industry and you need to keep abreast of the latest technology, realize that some of these technologies simply disrupt the way one person communicates with another. Two people that are sitting next to each other can give each other thousands of communication signals by either their body language, appearance, actions or their words.

For you to pick up the phone and give someone a call to tell them something very simple may take less than 60 seconds. However, let's say you decide to use e-mail to try to tell that person something. In order for you to type that 60 second message, you may need to dial up (well, maybe you have DSL) open your email program or browser, input in your user name and password, wait for approval, insert in their email address, a subject line, type in your message, proof read it quickly and then hit send. This process alone can easily take up to ten minutes or more. Unless you mean to give 50 people the exact same message, and wish to copy everyone and then hit *send*, this form of communication is actually sucking time away from you.

To give you an example, a young lady that I know happens to have five separate e-mail accounts. She has an e-mail account for work, one for school, two for personal, one that she can retrieve Web based info, and another that she can retrieve only with her Outlook Explorer, and the last one that she sends her junk mail to. And she opens, reads and goes through them all once, sometimes twice a day. She spends an estimated 5 to 10 minutes per e-mail account checking and responding every day. In addition to this, she has her home answering machine, her cell phone voicemail, and her work answering service. During work, she has her friends instant message her through AOL, sending her attachments or links to Web sites with their pictures on them. All told, these *advanced* forms of communication—all of which have no relation to her home-based business—costs her an estimated 2 to 3 hours daily. Does this situation ring all too familiar for you?

So what to do? List all the devices and communication methods that you utilize on a weekly basis so that you understand what they are and how they relate to your actual business life. Then begin eliminating some of these methods of communication that are no longer empowering you. To put it succinctly, *Keep It Simple*, Smartguy!

Two Theories on Managing Your Time

There are two concepts at hand in being able to manage and juggle the limited amount of time that we have each day. The first is obvious, "what people are trying to do." What they are trying to do is, convince themselves that they will be able to "stretch" their mind and handle more things, by using more and more of these ways to communicate with the other human beings. In theory, believing that by simply exercising the brain as you would a muscle, it will become stronger and stronger. More specifically, believing that your mind will be able to handle more multitasking and management, and be able to balance work and play. Theoretically yes, if you stretch and grow your brain. To be putting demands on it that are way beyond what is currently demanded out of you, your brain will be able to hold more information, process more information, and become more powerful and potentially be able to be tapped beyond the 3%, that we all hear about. (There is a theory that humans only use 3% of their brain's potential.)

The second concept is the belief that you are not an effective enough being. Thus, you sometimes need to be able to use simple tricks to make your job easier. Although I believe in striving, excelling, and fulfilling your potential, I'm presenting this program to help you accomplish your financial potential as quickly as possible.

All of my life, speed was of the essence. I wanted to accomplish as much as I could before my ten-year high school reunion—including making over a million dollars a year. Therefore I would like to present to you, the way that I did it. The way that works best for me takes less than a minute to learn, if that. Unfortunately, this simple technique took me several years to be able to *master*. But this was because, since the technique is so simple, I would forget to do it the first thing in the morning *every day*. Without a doubt, I know that if I had practiced it daily, I could have mastered it in half the time.

My technique is nothing new. It is not something revolutionary, nor is it a secret. I'm just presenting to you what has worked for me. If you asked some other entrepreneur, they may suggest something else. For example, some other entrepreneur might say, "I absolutely could not have been able to accomplish everything that I have, as well as manage my entire business without this Palm Pilot," or "without Post It Notes and a cork board." That person will tell you what was important for him or her. I am just presenting what was important to me—what I needed to do everyday, and what I currently do everyday to run my companies.

First, *assume that your brain is not efficient*. By that I mean do not try to use this technique by committing things to memory. You will need to write things down—and again, because I cannot stress this enough, you will need to do this every single day.

Six Things To Do

There are so many programs out there regarding *time management*. People have Outlook, Palm Pilots, Franklin Covey organizers, Tony Robins even has a time management system. They are all good. I have studied them all and what I've chosen to use is a very simple system called "Six Things." Six Things is a system employing a calendar, with a space for each date that is large enough for you to be able to write one good-sized paragraph. I do not recommend anything smaller. But the calendar itself needs to be able to fit inside a small three-ring binder that can be carried around with you no matter where you go, without being bulky or cumbersome. The organizer that I carry with me is no bigger than 5" by 8" and no thicker than three-quarters of an inch. The calendar is toward the back and some simple lined papers are toward the front. The organizer does not have *any* business cards, credit cards, pockets or places to put change. And the reason for this specification is that it needs to feel almost like a wallet. Sometime in the past you may have written down a grocery list, or your "things to do" list on a scrap of paper and ended up carrying that list with you in your back pocket. And every time you forget what else you had to do that day, you simply pulled that list out of your back pocket and looked at it. That is how this organizer needs to function.

This is my trick. There are memory courses and various tricks, or mnemonics, to make your brain work. These tricks do not actually make your brain work better. However what I believe they do is relieve the mind of the clouds and the confusion, and allow you to think more creativity and concentrate on what is most important to you. You can focus on what you really want to do in that day and what you really want to get out that day. Because you are using this technique every single day, to your peers you'll almost seem superhuman. Ideas will be flowing out of you, you can remain calm at all times regardless of whatever chaos may be going on around you at your work. You'll be able to accomplish so much more within such a short amount of time. You will have this journal, and when you look back at what was accomplished over the past month or six months, you'll be astounded. You and others around you will have noticed a significant difference. The changes that you had hoped to see in yourself will have actually come to pass. Almost as if they were wishes that you had given to a Genie in a lamp.

There are those people who are never able to get anything done. There are those who have all the degrees, all the intelligence, the creativity, yet they are not able to accomplish all that much in their day-to-day life. They had all the resources, they networked well, and were the ones who should have been able to handle everything, but were just not able to. Why? They are bogged down with so much information and not a clue as to how to apply it toward an end product or goal.

So I repeat, no matter how good you think your memory is, assume your brain is not efficient. That is my program. I just assume that I am not that smart and that I cannot remember anything. Factual information, appointments, phone numbers I assume I will forget. And I make it okay in my mind to be forgetful. That frame of mind eases my brain. Maybe the only thing that I do try to remember within the 30 minutes that I spend with someone at a party or some other social setting would be a name. Other than that, a *business contact* that I meet at a conference table is instantly written down in the folder I have in front of me. If it relates to business, I write everything down.

For my business information (data regarding a specific type of information or project) I use Manila folders with lined paper inside them. All addresses are kept within a simple excel file (a contact management software may also be used). But don't use more than one place to record your addresses. I have seen people who keep some numbers in business card holders, more numbers in their organizers, other numbers are only stored on their cell phone—numbers that they have half at the office, half at home, etc. What happens is, when they think of someone they need to contact, they go on a long drawn-out mental search of where they should begin to look in order to find that information. Don't do that. Have all your contact info in one place or file.

Once you have your pocket-sized organizer, it's time to apply the Six Things technique. The technique is very simple. First thing when your day begins, come up with six things you are going to accomplish. Make sure at least one or two involve your financial goal. Regardless of how easy a task is to do that day and no matter how simple you think it will be to accomplish, you will need to write it down on your "Six Things to Do Today" list. Finally, and this is very important, complete one before you do another. That is about it.

When Contingencies Arise

Throughout the day, you may think of something that you did not realize that you needed to do that day. If this happens, stop what you're doing. Open up your binder, and write it down. Then at that point do what is most important first and complete it before you go on to the next. If you believe the new task that you have is more important than the one that you are currently working on, then make a conscious decision that you are going to stop working on the current project and begin working on the new task at hand, making sure you complete it before you go back to the other. Some people stop doing one task and begin another they just remembered that they needed to do. The result is the day will go by and they will have done all six things inefficiently or partially, and yet never finished any one of them.

The result of completing one task before moving on to the next may be that you will have completed possibly only one or two things on your list for that day. However, they will have been completed and finished. This has become my cornerstone in managing my time.

I've seen it time and time again. People will think, "I don't have that much to do today," and they don't make their "Six Things" list. Even if you only have one thing you absolutely need to do that day, you need to stay in the habit of always making your daily list. People will say, "I only need to do one thing today, so I don't need to write it down." They end up all day long trying to remember to do that one simple thing, or getting distracted from doing it. Then they'll remember a second thing that they need to do that day and they fail to write this other thing down. So now they are trying to remember to get to two things that they need to do that day. They go back and forth. "Let's see, I need to do number one, and I needed to do number two." That process envelopes them throughout the entire day—and then a third thing comes up. Now the pattern repeats. And the task of remembering more and more things becomes difficult—let alone trying to recall six things throughout a day. Or trying to recall what you were doing yesterday, or last week in working toward your goal. However, you then realize you never actually finished that task, so you were going to work on it this week…

I hope by now you see my point—you will use up your mental resources *recalling* tasks and not accomplishing them. The effort of trying to remember the days and the things to do robs the mind of its creativity and innovation, and you end up being confused, frustrated and unproductive. It could be something as simple as going to the grocery store, paying a bill, remembering to register for this one class, or to make this one important phone call today. Don't debate with yourself how simple this or that task is to remember. Just write it down, and be sure to finish one task before you go on to another.

How to Begin Creating Wealth Without Quitting Your Job

This is a very powerful way of using your time effectively and efficiently. Most Americans have a 9-to-5 job. They are working anywhere from 40 to 50 hours a week. They may have ambition and goals set, however they are not able to get to where they really want to be financially. This is because they are not able to devote a certain amount of time each week to a potentially big moneymaking project.

As an example, in *Diagram One* on the next page, you see a circle with a "$" sign in it representing a mainstream of income that you may currently have. This may be your current job, or something that you need to do every single week in order to continue your income stream. If you are a student and you are getting your finances from student loans, a guardian or parents, this counts too.

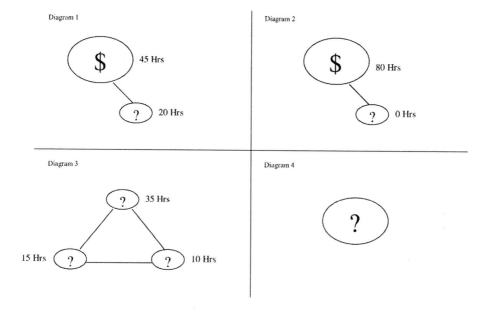

Diagram 1

$ 45 Hrs

? 20 Hrs

Diagram 2

$ 80 Hrs

? 0 Hrs

Diagram 3

? 35 Hrs

15 Hrs ?

? 10 Hrs

Diagram 4

?

For simplicity we'll call this your *job*. This is something that you need to do every single week. Let's say you devote 45 hours a week to your current job. If you take on another project and do not know if this is going to succeed or fail—create an income stream or not—you may wish to devote, let's say, 20 hours a week to your project. This would be your ideal situation in *Diagram One*.

I have built a thriving business using *Diagram One*, by having a steady job and building a small business on the side, knowing that there is a steady stream of income I can always count on. Great capitalists have also built subsidiary companies using this technique. An example on a smaller scale would be a direct marketer recognizes that his or her side business was generating 50 percent of income as their traditional job, yet was taking them 1/5 the amount of time. That was when they decided to quit their primary job and go full-time into their secondary business. Those numbers will vary based on your comfort level. Some people will say, "I will not quit my steady, secure job until my side business is generating at least 100 percent as much income or more." Again, it is totally up to your comfort level when you decide to make your secondary your primary.

Diagram Two is an example of where your job takes up anywhere from 60 to 80 hours a week, or more. In this situation, your income may not even be secure enough. And if you fall under working those amounts of hours each week your income will be totally insufficient. In this situation, it is very difficult to take on a new project and you are truly in a dilemma where you do not have enough time. If this is your situation, I would not advise you to try a side business until you can somehow reduce your weekly hours and still bring home the necessary income. It isn't that I do not believe in working long hours. There is no sense in working for someone or a company that is not getting you to where you want to go. This is a situation where you are severely limited because you are trading all of your time for very little money. Or you may be trading your time for an average or slightly above average income. And this program is not about showing you techniques that will give you only slightly above-average results.

Diagram Three is where I see a lot of people. This is a situation where people who fear they won't have enough bring themselves into this particular dilemma. They choose to pursue three different projects—none of which has a steady income, and the inexperienced person is trying to juggle the time in between them. In this example, they may spend 35 hours a week on project one, 15 hours a week on project two, and 10 hours a week on project three. Of course, the person is not disciplined enough to set those hours aside and be dedicated to them, so they continually rotate. The next week they may spend 35 hours on project two, and only two hours on project one, and zero hours on project three. And so on.

This diagram also may represent someone who has a steady job. So project one is their steady job. Their income does not fluctuate and they are spending 35 to 40 hours a week on that project. However, they choose to take on two or three other projects, again trying to juggle time between the two. I am very familiar with starting a small side business. Twenty hours a week for a side project is pretty much the standard commitment. And that would leave plenty of time to also be able to have a family life, a steady stream of income, as well as your new opportunity. So if you have only 20 hours a week for your side project and the inexperienced person is splitting that 20 hours a week into two or three separate projects. This is a perfect example where they may feel like they are doing a lot of things, but will never complete the project, or make any decent money.

Diagram Four is an example of where you go into a business with no safety net. This is the most aggressive type of approach to pursuing any opportunity where you will either sink or swim. With this approach to a project, obviously you absolutely do not know whether this opportunity will make any money—yet you do not have a steady stream of income or anything else as a back up. Be careful if you try this. It may move quickly to become Diagram Three, especially in the beginning. When pursuing such a venture, some people start having self-doubts. Especially after the first year, they may begin looking at other opportunities and stray away from what they had set out to accomplish initially. It is very easy for them to become Diagram Three where they take on one or two more projects, just to feel safe. Again, without having a steady steam of income, nor set hours, basically the second project is taking away from the first one. Diagram Four can also evolve into Diagram Two where you are working 60, 80 or 100 plus hours a week on your sole project. However, sometimes this particular project does not end up being the opportunity that you had initially sought—or the industry changes. Thus, you are working harder at the same project, the opportunity develops a ceiling, and you're always making the same amount of money, with a grim future.

Here is an example. Back in the '80s real estate was a hot market—whether people got into the real estate industry as an investor, salesperson, developer, or whatever. People were making an amazing return on their investments, whether it was their time or their money. When the "bottom fell out" and the industry changed, opportunities were no longer as lucrative, and people ended up having to work more hours and got paid less.

Another example that I am personally familiar with is the telecom industry. I was in a telecom sales organization and the opportunities back in the '90s were exploding, with the deregulation and along with the Internet. However as telecom companies started going through price wars and mergers, again, the opportunities became less lucrative. Therefore, when I was in the industry, that project began for me as a Diagram Four. Eventually it had evolved, through no fault of mine to a Diagram Two.

Diagram Four may be something that you wish to do. It is the most aggressive and courageous way of approaching business where you very strongly believe in your abilities. I have done that a few times in the past. But I do not advise that *everyone* try the experience of Diagram Four—and definitely not everyone will wish to. It requires an unwavering constitution in the face of great adversity. Then again, *Great* leaders and capitalist have emerged from using this approach to business.

No one way is better than the other. It all depends on the individual and his or her ability to be able to effectively balance projects—and it depends on your comfort level. If you are just beginning your first business opportunity, I would recommend going with Diagram One. It will put you and your family in a comfortable situation and can help you clear your mind as you pursue your opportunity. It can also help you balance your life with work, love, and play. If you have a decent job, I wouldn't go out and quit tomorrow because you stumbled upon an opportunity. Work your job. But also realize it is only job and only means to an end.

Remember to do your *Six Things* that you need to do that day. Be aggressive, but at the same time, be realistic. Don't put anything outrageous on your list like, "I'm going to get the CEO of this major billion dollar Corporation to personally fund my new project today." I don't know, you may be able to do that. But please, do simple, basic things that you need to do each day that will get you closer to your goal. And remember to complete at least one each day.

Also remember, when you decide on your project and you write your *Six Things* list, either right next to it or at least at end of the week, put down the amount of hours that you will absolutely devote to this project. And of course, make sure that some of your *Six Things* are working toward your goals. Every morning as you see your *bathroom goals* list, one of those six things should be an action that you gets you closer to accomplishing one of them. If you have three to five things that you need to complete before the end of this year, using some of these techniques within this session will be helpful, such as completing one before you move onto another—understanding that when it comes to your year or your three to five year goal, that it may not be as simple as completing one before the other. Still, remember to focus on completing more of one and at least being able to check off one of your *bathroom goals* as "finished."

8

Delegation

The final thing that you absolutely need in order to be successful, is knowing how to leverage your own activities, otherwise known as delegation. Delegation is an advanced form of time management. Although you can learn how to do one without learning the other, these two forms of taking your abilities to the maximum work the best when they go hand-in-hand.

Delegation as a definition is when one or more persons is appointed or chosen, and commissioned to represent another. As capitalists have said during the Industrial Revolution, "I would much rather get 1% out of 100 of my men than have to get the 100% from myself." And that phrase alone is extremely powerful. Although I had heard it for several years and had been told by many managers that phrase was extremely important, it was only when I had worked with larger and larger organizations, and ultimately built my own company, when it really clicked for me. The meaning is simple and it does not take hours to analyze. It simply means rather than working yourself to death, it is much easier to have 100 people doing a portion of the job.

And this is where I hear close-minded people intone, "Well, that is easy for *you* to say. You have the money to pay for a hundred people to work for you. Where am I going to get the money to hire somebody? If I had the money or the people to work for me, I wouldn't be in my current situation." If you approach this concept with a poor person's mentality, you will be correct, you'll never get anybody to work for you, or with you. The hardest part about this technique that you need to master, is to first except its simplicity, yet powerfulness. By doing so, what you've opened your eyes to, are the obvious possibilities that there are—especially in this day and age where you have the opportunity to have people work with you as a team.

Diagram Five is a simple illustration representing the previous technique of time management. It looks like a pie. You have six things that you need to do that day. And all delegation is, is to take one piece of that pie and have someone else do it.

Diagram 5

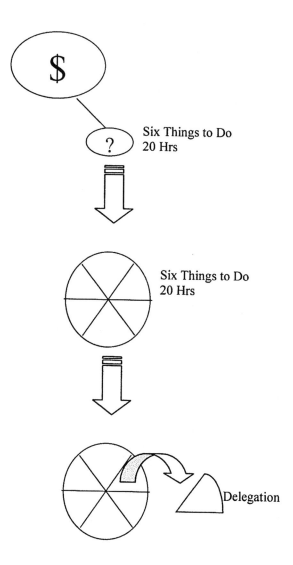

Six Things to Do
20 Hrs

Six Things to Do
20 Hrs

Delegation

That is about it. If you learn how to start off with this simple technique, what you are then doing is freeing up some of your time, and you start leveraging someone else's efforts to your advantage. When you begin using this pie example daily, it will get you closer to getting that "1% out of 100 people" theory. Remember, take baby steps in the beginning.

Automatic Bill Pay

One way you can delegate your time is through the modern miracle of electronics. Your bank or an online service offers an automatic bill paying system that you can use for zero or a very small monthly service fee. Paying bills once or twice a month can easily add up to three to eight hours a month—especially if you are trying to pay different bills on different dates, and clouding the mind trying to remember what days to make your payments. Even if there is a nominal service fee it is very well worth it. With an automatic bill paying system it's as if you have a personal secretary paying all of your bills for you. This alone can free up hours of your time without costing you very much money—or no money. Add to that the once or twice that you miss the deadline on paying some of your credit card bills, factor in the penalty and late fees, and the peace of mind is well worth it. Signing up is something you do once, and your bills are paid on time from then on.

Don't Burn Out

The reason delegation is so important is that no matter how much a person has mastered time management, and is able to work efficiently at all times, there is still a limited amount of time that one has to dedicate to work. What is the maximum that a person can work in a single day? It is 24 hours. And even if you were working all 24 hours a day, there are only so many days that you can do that until you burn out. You hear about doctors, attorneys or business owners who work 80, 100, 120 hours a week. The maximum that they can work in a single day is 24 hours. That is the total amount of effort that they can supply. With delegation, you get what you make, plus, you are able to get an override, or some sort of income or benefit from someone else's effort, even if that is just one other person. What if you had three people working for you? Not you working crazy hours such as 24 hours in a single day. Instead, they are working 8 hours a day. How many hours a day are you benefiting from? The 24 hours.

At that point, do you even need to work? This is where people start to understand delegation and learn how to leverage themselves. It begins with this process. They understand that there is a limitation on their personal ability. They understand that they need to build a team and to keep a team happy. That way, even when they are not working themselves, personally, they are benefiting from others. Obviously this is not where they stop. They continually recruit more and more people and build teams. What if they have six people working for them? Twelve? Twenty-four people? A lot of small businesses do. The business owner is now benefiting from 192 hours a day of someone else's efforts. That is almost 1,000 hours a week. Understanding this will help you to realize the importance of recruiting people to build a team with, whether they are partners, companies, employees, independent contractors, or salespeople. As long as they are people who you can comfortably work with.

Some people will say, "I can't even imagine 100 people working for me, whether they are employed directly by me or self-employed." During the Industrial Revolution, these railroad, oil or steel tycoons had thousands of men working for them. The technology we have nowadays has allowed us to shorten the distance between two people with the telephone and modem. So if you are not able to imagine 100 people, would it be possible to see yourself working with 10? Ten people who are all trying to achieve the same or a similar goal. And even though those 10 people may not be able to commit 100 percent of their time to work for you or with you, could it be possible for them commit 10 percent each? What you have done is you've now multiplied yourself. Even if everyone is only giving 10 percent, that equals over 100 percent of effort. So if one person gets sick, loses interest or for some reason does not participate in the program, the whole company does not go down. But if you're the type who feels like you need to do everything, because "no one does it better than you," that's where you become vulnerable. You're running around, giving 110 percent, burning yourself out and, God forbid, if something were to happen to you, the company immediately stops running.

This is a reason why I am a big fan of network marketing companies. Although lately it has not been as lucrative as it has been in the past, if you join a network marketing or a multilevel marketing company, you can experience the delegation concept working right in front of you. You have a group of members who all get together with the same goal in mind. People put into the program the amount of effort that they can spare, because most people start on a part-time basis, attempting to supplement their current income. And the incentive is that eventually you can have over 100 people working with you, and you get an override on the income that they make. Since most of these companies are a commission based program, the people who work for you do not get paid unless they sell something.

Take a moment and think about how you can benefit from this particular delegation concept. Could you utilize this method? If you are either starting your own company or starting a distributorship program, you have people work for you or help to market the products or services on a commissioned basis. Many large multiple billion dollar corporations have built up their sales force this way.

Let's say you are going to get into real estate investing. A real estate agent is a perfect example of where someone is hunting for investment properties for you for free. And you do not need to pay them until they find you a profitable investment property. They are your eyes and ears for your real estate business. However, you need to understand that you only need to recruit them. It does not take money for them to begin working for you. You just need to be able to communicate your idea of the future with them, so that you are not the only one scouring the newspapers and the Internet for a good deal. They are doing the looking for you. Could you get more than one agent? Sure you can. Serious real estate investors have 10, 20, 30 or more agents and brokers looking for deals and presenting them to the investor. And the investor is constantly recruiting more.

When I had built up my company I continued to outsource the tasks that needed to be done. For example, if I needed someone to do data entry, I would use people who wanted to work out of their own home and they would e-mail their work daily to our office. They got paid on a per-entered basis. When we needed a project manager, rather than hiring someone, training them, and hoping that they knew what they were doing, we decided to outsource that activity to a company where they were accountable. They made a percentage of the business that they managed. For our accounting, rather than hiring a bookkeeper to work in-house we chose to drop off monthly files to a local accounting company. Through all this outsourcing we had at times over 100 people working for the company but not particularly inside our office. Using this method, we were networked with independent contractors in other states. We had experts working in each department and had room for expansion. Because they were hired for a short ramp up time, we were able to keep the overhead low. People or companies were paid on performance, they were not just sitting around collecting a paycheck.

Entrepreneur Story

Minh Le' s story is an excellent example of using delegation to succeed. Minh was going to college and was not looking forward to sitting in a cubicle, grinding out reports after he graduated. He wasn't quite sure what he wanted to do, however he knew that what he did not want to do was to work for someone else. One of the things that he *did* like doing was playing video games online. If you're not familiar with this, it is where you are playing a game with people in other parts of the world, connecting at real-time with a modem. For instance, if you are playing a marksman type of a game where you are trying to "shoot" each other for points, you can be in Wisconsin and "shoot" someone who is online and playing the very same game in London.

The game that Minh liked to play was very popular, had lots of fans, and on any given night there were literally thousands of people playing the game against each other on the Internet. And the company that created this game allowed people to make changes to the game and customize it for themselves. Minh decided that he wanted to create his *own* game using the concept of the old one. Since the game that was popular at the time had a huge following of enthusiasts, there were plenty of people who wanted to help out, just because of their love of playing this type of game. Over the Internet he was able to recruit people who knew how to customize an interactive game. He had certain people create different types of weapons, characters, and scenes or plot options.

So rather than Minh every night frantically trying to program or invent a new game all by himself in his parents' basement, he was able to get other people involved and leverage himself by *delegating* some of the programming. What he was able to do was to see the opportunity as well as utilize the Internet and connect himself with other people. After several months of collaboration, the game that was co-created was called *Counter Strike*. This game ended up generating over $40 million in sales.

9

THE APPRENTICE Can Help You Succeed

I have always had a huge thirst for knowledge, but I've had to overcome the daunting challenge that reading has been for me since my youth. Then, I discovered the educational TV channels such as History, Nova, Discovery, A&E, MSNBC, etc. They were able to give me almost as much information in an hour as reading and discussing a chapter in a textbook, which might take me a week or two. A one-hour show regarding how the creation of a black hole was created in the universe, explained me in much more than a convoluted 20 pages of text and 4 or 5 pictures in a thick $70 textbook. A documentary on the Civil War and how it came to be, on the History channel, explained it to me in much more vivid details, than I would have gotten from reading a few chapters and listening to a teacher standing front of 40–60 students reiterating the chapter in his or her own words.

Up until recently, there have been only three types of television shows that featured segments devoted to the discussion of achieving personal wealth. First there were shows such as CNBC, MSNBC and the financial networks. Secondly, shows on A&E, Biography, or the History Channel have showcased the biographies of famous capitalists and industrialists, such as Rockefeller, Hershey and Ford. They tell the history of capitalism in this country, featuring people who grew from humble beginnings to become self-made millionaires or the today's equivalent billionaires. These stories are my personal favorites because I can learn from these entrepreneurs who took great risks in the late 1800s and early 1900s. I'm amazed at how they were able to organize tens of thousands of workers and develop huge industries without the use of computers or the technology we have today. And third are the late night infomercials, which oftentimes are ridiculed by most of us. And now, network television has embraced and transformed the idea of educating as well as providing entertainment with the offering of "reality television" and a show called "The Apprentice."

The Apprentice

In it's first season, *The Apprentice* was the #1 new show on television, with an average of 20.7 million people tuning in to watch every week. Executive produced by and starring Donald Trump, eighteen candidates were split into two teams. Each week, Trump had them endure rigorous business tasks while living together in a Manhattan loft apartment. The candidates, who were relatively successful in their own careers, came to New York to go through a 13-week grueling and intensive "job interview," in order to hopefully claim their prize of working for Trump.

Prominent Fortune 500 companies were enlisted to provide many of the tasks. The tasks tested the candidates' intelligence and street smarts. They faced the challenges of living in close quarters, completed difficult job assignments, and were forced to think "outside the box" in order to outshine each other and get to the top. Every episode began with a task assignment and ended with a climactic boardroom showdown. Each week, one candidate was sent home in a taxi, right after he or she heard, "You're Fired!" by Donald Trump. The winner of the competition became Trump's "apprentice" and was granted the dream job of a lifetime within The Trump Organization at a hefty six-figure salary.

This show was an opportunity for the public to now see how success and financial excellence can be achieved when individuals vigorously apply themselves. Success was no longer touted as being "lucky." Nor was it attributed to the cliché, "It's not *what* you know, it is *who* you know." This cliché has become a mantra for many individuals who simply do not apply themselves, because they feel that they do not "know *anyone*," so why bother? Thus, instead of putting forth any real effort, they settle themselves into that "comfort zone" of an excuse to not try and do anything special, but just get by.

The Apprentice has really broken new ground by demonstrating, through the arduous tasks that the candidates had to do, what entrepreneurs who achieve wealth must do. Very few highly successful people just became "lucky," or invented a great idea. Most are hard-working individuals who have learned to apply themselves, delegate authority, and have accepted and applied the basic principles of business. And this was accomplished with information that has always been available to everyone.

The Apprentice did not take people who were failing in life and magically change them 180 degrees—which is usually the theme on moneymaking infomercials. Nor did the show take a rags-to-riches type of approach. It was an eye-opener for most people as well as being educational, when the contestants were people who had either excelled academically and/or in business.

I appreciated the fact that they had chosen the best of the best as candidates—individuals who were willing to "get off the couch" in order to have a lifestyle of wealth and power. This was not the typical showcase where you see individuals who have no business being in business, and are looking to "strike it rich" as we generally see on game shows, or on the weekly announcement of lotto winners, or on infomercials. Oftentimes television game shows deliberately choose "average" individuals who appeal to the mass media. Their charm being that they are "everyday" mid-to-low economic class people who have miraculously found themselves on a show such as this. The public seems to love stories like the Vegas tourist who hit the jackpot, or the depressed single mother who wins the lotto because she just happened to buy a ticket that week. Good for Trump to not play it safe and just select that stereotype for his show.

The reason I bring this up is that I often encounter young people and students who wish to do nothing on their part, yet want me to provide them with the "holy grail" to personal wealth. People have asked me, "So, if I just read your book, I will get rich, right?" Trying not to insult them (or lose a potential fan), I say, "No. Reading it will do nothing. But *applying* it does!" Likewise, when it comes to *The Apprentice*, watching the show will do nothing. Only applying the techniques that are presented will. If you can grasp that concept, you can go beyond "average" and achieve whatever you want to.

In this book, I have given you information on the importance of clearing your mind of the "garbage" or negativity that you may have been feeding it, then focusing on and setting goals, then using time management and delegation. Essentially, I am teaching you to crawl, then to learn how to walk and then run. A show such as *The Apprentice* can now show you how to run, sprint and win the race. Unfortunately, many people will say they want to win the race but they refuse to even learn how to walk, and remain in the world of crawlers. In many of his interviews, Trump has said that he did not wish to do a show that would break the integrity of what it takes to make it in big business and in New York. Although he did not select the candidates for the show, he promised that he would not keep someone on, or not fire someone, for the sake of good television.

The Lemonade Task

The first episode of *The Apprentice* began with the contestants waking up that morning not knowing what was in store for them. The contestants received a call from Trump's assistant instructing them to show up on the floor of the New York Stock Exchange. The contestants as well as the viewers were eager to find out what their very first task was going to be, as Trump stood on the famous NYSE balcony ready to announce what was going to begin the process of elimination.

What was on millions of viewers' minds—as well as the contestants, as they gathered at the New York Stock Exchange? Everyone probably had a grandiose idea of what the task was going to be. Were they going to run a startup company for a day? Work on a product launch for a multi-billion dollar corporation? No. What Donald Trump decided to start off with was to sell lemonade on the streets of New York. What an excellent choice!

It was great that Trump did not attempt to cater to those millions of people who have a false sense of what it takes to succeed, imagining the *fantasy* of what it takes to become an entrepreneur. Those ideas of, "When I become the boss, I'll get to tell everyone how it is, and order people around," or, "In order to be successful I need a pre-assembled team for me to do whatever I tell them to do, and get my coffee," were quickly extinguished after watching the first show. On the "Lemonade Stand" episode, Trump told the candidates that having the basics of salesmanship is a requirement in business and becoming successful, whether you like it or not. This became quickly obvious to contestants on the show who thought they were too good to go out and sell—not only to sell lemonade but to sell themselves. And of course, it was in one of the toughest markets to sell. It separated those who were not willing to do whatever it takes, or who believed that they were above selling lemonade on the streets of New York.

I was surprised at first that *The Apprentice* was as harsh as it is to the candidates, and that the viewers did not lose interest and switch channels to something that makes them feel better about themselves. I hope people are getting the message: this show really elevates individuals to where they have to be responsible to push themselves. In each episode, Trump has also taken a moment to talk directly to the viewers at home on techniques and philosophies in business and life. I hope that how the candidates challenge themselves and each other has awakened certain people who question themselves as to why they can't seem to find such opportunities, and realize it's because of their own lack of motivation and drive.

Donald Trump's *The Apprentice* is a big step in the right direction toward motivating the 20+ million viewers per week. I hope that *The Apprentice* and other shows such as this will continue to air and give insight into what it takes to enter the field of high-stakes business. Whether it is a reality show on what it takes to lose weight, become a model, enter the music industry, or whatever, television is now giving viewers real insight into what it *really* takes to be successful within those industries. And again, always placing the responsibility for success back on the person.

Week after week, Donald Trump's *The Apprentice* makes one thing perfectly clear: no one and no thing (i.e., gadget) is going to magically make you successful. There are no more excuses. Your success is up to you. It's not just a matter of working *harder*, you also have to start working *smarter*. And in these pages I'll show you how.

Parents and TV

For generations, parents and teachers have discouraged young individuals from entertainment, presented in the latest form of multimedia. They would talk about the 'old days' and how the use of imagination is a superior way of entertaining and feeding the mind. And educational? They felt television was never educational. In the beginning it was believed that, Rock and Roll, radio or record players were brainwashing the young, and were even messages from the devil himself. Then they came to view movies and television as devices that were basically designed to rot the brain. Now, obviously, surfing the net and chatting online is an activity that parents and teachers consider to be an entertainment medium, which will get young individuals nowhere. Although I may agree that several years ago television was a form of canned laughter entertainment that was just the manifestations of a bunch of starving writers in Hollywood, today multimedia communicates multi-sensorial, and that cannot be wrong.

They used to claim that the only way to get a true understanding of a subject was by reading about it. The information itself was pure, and not tainted by other factors or by Hollywood. They were clinging onto the old ways and traditions, and not understanding the basic human advancement of technology. They tried to simplify the message to the masses with 30-second Public Service Announcements whereas making celebrities simply become a parrot that don't even understand why or what message they are saying anymore. With messages such as "Stay in school! (So that you can get a good job.)" or "Reading is Learning." It is great that people are not left to become unskilled, illiterate, and a burden to society.

But, the message has often been interpreted as, "If you do not do well in school, you are destined for failure." Or, "If you have a difficult time reading, you cannot properly learn." This is not always true. If you have ever felt that way because a parent or teacher has ever said or implied that to you, you need to eradicate that message from your mind. Education can be obtained in many forms including and other than reading a book. And yes, I do realize I am saying this as you are *reading my book.*

Here's a simple illustration to support my point: many of you reading this chapter love music. You may appreciate how it makes you feel. You may like contemporary pop music, dance, hip-hop, country, classical, etc. Whatever your preference is, when you hear music that you enjoy, you truly feel within your heart how the music evokes a special feeling, emotion or inspiration. However, let's say the same individuals who have told us, "Reading is the only way to learn" all our lives, are now saying that the only way that you can appreciate music is by learning how to *read music* from sheets of paper. And, that you need to first learn how to read music notations, which may take several years. No, no, no. You can't just *listen* to it or *watch* a music video. That is taboo. You must first learn to read it, so that you can then imagine in your mind how it sounds. Only then could you appreciate what the original song writer was thinking, without the interpretations by other artists, such as the musicians, singers, audio mixer, music video director, etc. This has been the interpretation of multimedia education today by parents and teachers entrenched in the "old ways of learning."

But consider this: even a young child can learn how to hum a song, which they may have heard for the first time, within a few seconds or minutes. And even if the child is not particularly musically inclined, they would still be able to put variations on that music and make it their own, almost instantly. But the pompous academicians out there, would prefer to make this process cumbersome. They would much rather have the child learn to read the musical notes, learn to play an instrument, and then replay that tune precisely the same. All this so that the old school teachers of the world can grade them on how well that the child became a "tape recorder." They have taken the wonderful mind that can be inspired to create, and diminished it.

What is the point of all I am saying? The evolution of a new type of education has arrived. This is not to say that if you intend to learn music as a career, or to become an artist yourself, that you shouldn't study the fundamentals. But if anything inspires you, do not let anyone tell you that the only true way to learn and appreciate it is through the long intense study of the fundamentals, first. Instead, learn in *whatever* form inspires you first, whether it tingles your sight, sound, smell, touch or the *other* senses. Then decide for yourself if the right course of action for mastering your craft is intense academic study, or intense self-study.

If you are reading this book, you want to become rich; you do not want an average lifestyle. Well, the secret to becoming rich is not always accomplished by studying the fundamentals first. Meaning, if you do not do well in your math classes in high school, you get a 'D' in your first economics or business class you take in college, do not get discouraged. You will soon learn through your journey to wealth, that these fundamentals are actually better accomplished by delegating them to specialists. Delegate them to the kids that got all the 'A's in class, such as the accountants, business attorneys, consultants, etc., who you will eventually hire and have them work for you. Yes, understand that the fundamentals are important. But do not get caught up in the details or the cumbersome ways of taking in information. Keeping your focus on your primary talent and nurturing your determination is more important. If you are not good at math, it is okay to pick up a calculator or use the computer. If you can't read as well as others, you can learn through audio books or watch the documentary version. If you want to be rich, don't get caught up in just trying to perfect the fundamentals, such as the minute details of an Accounting 101 class. What do you want to end up doing, count other people's money? Realize the big picture. Determine and then focus on what will be the best course of action for you, that will keep you excited and get you closer to becoming rich.

The convergence of entertainment and education along with interactive multimedia is getting better all the time. And now boundless by physical locations, the future of education and learning has become very exciting. We are just at the tip of the iceberg with a show such as *The Apprentice*, where you are learning from an expert in an industry, in multimedia and multi-sensory form. This new form of education will not only be available at your local scheduled time on television, but will be soon be an 'on demand' information source at the touch of your keyboard, at any computer or digital device, anytime. The future of learning is just a keystroke away!

10

Infomercials and Multilevel Marketing Programs…Do They Work?

Many entrepreneurs have started with a home-based business. They may have started it in their garage, the den or the kitchen table. Entrepreneurs have built computers from their parents' basements, baked cookies in their home oven and sold them on a web site. Or designed popular games from their dorm room. All of these people built up a business and all starting from what they call their "home."

If you were to pick up a copy of *Entrepreneur magazine*, you will find several other types of home-based businesses listed. You can also start your own home-based business with the help of a company. The benefits of using an existing system is, they give you a guideline that you can follow—or modify and make it your own. It gives you a good starting point—a form of roadmap. This is where prepackaged home based businesses come in. These are programs that have been created to eliminate some of the guest work out of trying to start something from scratch.

You have probably seen all kinds of money-making programs. They have been coming at you and coming at you relentlessly. Either someone approached you, or you may have seen them through infomercials on television, or in newspapers, on the Internet, and through the mail. Or you may have gone in for what you thought was a job interview and it ended up being a "business opportunity." The line of questioning I get most often is, "Which one of these programs work? Are you really able to make the kind of money that they claim in their advertisements or sales pitch? Why or why not?"

Whenever a company or some person is trying to sell you on their "business opportunity" before you say yes, the main thing you need to determine is, "what is the potential?" We are in a time where not only a good idea, but the application of a good idea, can result in millions of dollars. First of all you need to ask yourself, "am I someone who can *apply* a good idea?"

To give you an example, is selling a cup of coffee a good idea? People have been selling cups of coffee for centuries. Ten years ago, if a company was selling you a business opportunity where you could sell cups of coffee for four or five dollars and told you that you'll make a lot of money, what would you think? Would you think, "Is there really potential in that business?" Would you think, "What if that business did not work for me?" Would you think that the company that sold you the business opportunity had probably sold you a deceptive business opportunity or a scam? However, a major billion dollar corporation was built on the concept of selling a cup of coffee. Think of Starbucks. Or various other successful franchises.

You may have seen infomercials or offers in the mail regarding buying real estate, or fixing them up and selling them, or rental properties, buying and selling cars, nutritional products, or mail order. Do people make money buying or selling real estate? Do people make money selling vitamins or nutritional products? Do people make money in mail order? The answer is yes. Of course they do. People in this country have built multibillion dollar industries with those simple categories.

Let's take real estate. I've actually met people who are so naïve, so close-minded, that they are of the opinion that you cannot make money in real estate in this country. They believe that any program or opportunity that is sold through infomercials or seminars that hype how the promoter made his or her money in real estate is just another deceptive opportunity to get money out of us honest Americans.

This country was built on opportunity seekers including real estate tycoons. The wealth built in New York or any other aggressive land purchases made by past Americans is a testament to any of that. Yet, these people who stay late up at night wondering why their life has not turned out the way they thought is was going to, are the ones who know better, right?

Can people make money in real estate? The answer is yes. These programs on how to make money in real estate that you may have seen on infomercials late at night, do they work?

The reality is some of these programs do work. Although there are the occasional ones that have blatantly falsified results, the majority of the programs that I have seen, and have attended myself, do work. But the reality is, 95% of the people who purchase these programs, do so because of their impulsive buying habit, compounded by their dire need to get out of a bad financial situation. Less than

5% of them will actually make the kind of money that the program's host is talking about. This is not because the information that was provided within the program is insufficient. Rather, the majority of the people who sign up for this type of program will not actually *apply* the information that is provided. They'll either talk themselves out of it, or they'll read the first chapter and decide not to go any further—or they'll realize that it's not as easy as they initially thought it was. The question you want answered is, "Will it work for *me?*"

Since this is the question that many people who want to start a home-based business ask, I would like to begin with a clean slate and explain how many of these programs work. In the next two sections, we will go over many of the popular moneymaking opportunities that are available—whether they are on television, something you got in the mail, or someone that you know approached you with it.

Oftentimes, people are looking for opportunities, but do not know what will be required of them or do not understand the intricacies of how these programs work. Some people have spent two, three, four, five years simply trying to figure out how these programs work. This section will identify many of those popular programs out there that you are most likely to encounter, so you can determine early on if it is something that you wish to do.

If, after going through this section, you realize that you do not wish to pursue the material from companies that market in this way, you will have saved an enormous amount of time on *trial and error* that I have seen other people go through. If you get confronted, or see an opportunity that has been explained in these two sections, you will be in a more educated position to make a rational decision. And you will *not* be just a negative person who thinks that there are absolutely no opportunities left, and that all these companies want to do is steal money from you.

What happens with many people is, they do not understand how the opportunity works, yet they discard it as "too good to be true." They'll say, "if it were so good, then *everyone* would be doing it." They make these comments because they are *scared.* Nine times out of ten, they did not actually evaluate the program—or by nature they are a negative person. This section is intended to get you to a place where if you decide something is not for you, it is only because you understand and are aware of the potential and the risks, and simply do not wish to pursue it.

The opportunities covered in these two sections are not the only types of home-based businesses. There are many types of home-based businesses that are not going to be covered in this section. I am focusing on the ones that circulate quite often, or are sold in large numbers, so if you have not already, you will hear a similar pitch sometime in the future.

Television Infomercials that Promise Riches, Do They Work?

You are restless one evening. You see that there is nothing to watch on the cable movie channels or the local channels. You start randomly flipping through the channels hoping to find something that can possibly inspire you or make you feel like you are in another time or place. Especially another adventure. Then you come across an infomercial.

This infomercial promises to free you. This is a freedom that you can acquire by purchasing their program. It sounds like as soon as you purchase this program that you will become instantly wealthy. Is this true? The truth is that the advertiser will do whatever it takes within legal guidelines to make a sale. You will end up filling in the blanks with what the advertiser does not say in order for you to believe, and basically get a sale. When you see an infomercial, what a lot of people do is they mentally put themselves in the place of the characters that are giving the testimonials. They will believe that they themselves are in this exact situation, and if they buy this program, they will get exactly what the person in the testimonial has.

To give an example, very many of these infomercials will portray a couple or an individual who was not satisfied with their life. After ordering and receiving the advertised program, they were able to accomplish what most Americans desire: financial freedom. People who see this type of advertisement commonly put it in their own minds that all they need to do is purchase the program that is offered in the advertisement and they will immediately experience the results of the individuals giving the testimonials.

Many people who watch these infomercials imagine the path to success. They'll believe that by simply giving their credit card to the order taker, they have launched themselves onto a path of financial success. They come to the conclusion that because they gave out their credit card number to the order taker, that they have done their part, and the rest is up to the advertiser to make it magically happen for them. And when they don't become rich overnight, they will then put the blame on the advertiser. Although this concept may sound silly to you, this is the mentality of many of the people who are pursuing financial freedom. They actually believe that the *responsibility* of amassing wealth is on another company or another person.

Many of these people have used their credit card to order TV offers before. Perhaps they bought jewelry on the Home Shopping Network. After all, when you use your credit card to order, it arrives in a week or two and you feel good. And you don't have to do anything to feel good except to open the package and put on the jewelry. They mistakenly apply this situation to financial success infomercials. They think they should be able to just open the package and instantly start experiencing wealth.

What is the reality? The reality is that the infomercials offer a vehicle that needs to be *used* to be successful. What they offer is *information* that has been used by other people who have made a considerable amount of money in the past using these particular techniques. What they are using is information in a form that is easily absorbed and user-friendly. The vast majority of people could not read a thick novel cover to cover that is over 400 or 500 pages within a day or two. Most people don't have the discipline to do so. However, most individuals would be able to comprehend the interpretation of the novel within a couple of hours at a local movie theater. The weeks that it would take to read a novel are condensed and presented to an individual within a couple of hours.

The information that these infomercial advertisers are providing you is something that may be available at your local bookstore. But it is has been condensed, repackaged and presented in a different way. Hopefully, an easier way. An easier way does not mean that you take the information, do nothing, and something great happens in your life. The information that is provided is information that is applicable and they have testimonials of people who have *applied* the information, meaning that they did not purchase that information just to hold onto it and hope for good results to magically materialize. What kind of person are you?

What do you think is the longest-running infomercial? It is not Ron Popeil's "Set It And Forget It" rotisserie oven, or Richard Simmons' "Sweating To The Oldies" video tapes, or George Foreman's Grill. It is a moneymaking program by Carlton Sheets. He sells his system on how to buy real estate investment properties all across country using his *no money down* system. He has numerous testimonies from people who have had success using his program.

Yet this is where I hear a lot of people saying that the program does not work. Hundreds of thousands have bought his system. Obviously there is a market for people who have become sick and tired of going to their day-to-day jobs. Does that mean hundreds of thousands of people are becoming rich? Does that mean, "Well if it were really that easy *everyone* would be doing it?" No. Why? Because of the contingency I mentioned before. Some will apply it and some won't. Does that mean it does not work? The man has been a real estate investor for decades.

He has been selling his program for over 14 years. And if his program did not really work, if it was a total rip-off, he obviously would have been shut down by the FTC. Have people purchased real estate properties in this country without anything down? The answer is yes. People do that all the time, with or without Carlton's system. Is Carlton showing you a method on how people have purchased real estate properties with nothing down? The answer is again yes.

So, whether you have seen an infomercial on how you can make money in real estate, buying and selling on E-bay, or mail order, and you are thinking of buying a system you saw on television or at a seminar, the answer in general regarding moneymaking infomercials is, that *yes*, they provide very good information and they do work, *if you can apply them*. The bottom line is, it's up to *you*. Do you have the drive and the perseverance to succeed? Are you the type who will stay the course, or will you get quickly bored or impatient and quit?

Multilevel Marketing

A friend who you haven't talked to in awhile calls you up out of the blue and excitedly says, "You need to come see this. What time can I pick you up? Are you available this Thursday at 7:00? Great, I will come pick you up." He's acting kind of strange. You ask him what it is. He says, "I can't explain it, you have to see it, so can I pick you up at 7:00?"

Or, you may have seen a flyer posted on a message board. It may have said something along the lines of, "Make $500 to $1,000 a week, no experience necessary." You go in for what you thought was an interview with a resume in hand and all of a sudden you're in a room with lots of other people. Smiling people come up to you, introducing themselves, telling you how much success they've had in the company. Or they may explain to you that this or that person has become one of the youngest directors.

No one wants to see your resume. They ask you to sit down along with the rest of the group. A guy enthusiastically jumps up in front of the room and starts telling a rags-to-riches story. He talks about the poor job market and the way the economy is going. He tells a story that may sound similar to your story. He talks about not being able to find a job that would pay him well or that there was a corporate ceiling. And then he discovered this company. And the company has provided him with unlimited opportunities and financial freedom. Come join our company and you can get rich too!

So what happened? You have been hit by a multilevel company. The concept of multilevel marketing is nothing more than a sales organization where you are paid on commission only. You also get an "override commission" on sales made from people that you recruit into the company. Other than that, there is no mystery about these types of organizations. They often use different names and different pitches so that people don't understand immediately that it is essentially a sales job or a part-time sales business. They may use terms at this meeting such as, "this is my *partner,* my *team,* or my *upline.*" If you are not familiar, an *upline* is the person or persons directly above them in a multilevel commission structure.

Other types of sales organizations also use similar types of commission structures. Financial, real estate or insurance companies use a similar payout plan in that they offer you opportunities where you work on a commission-only basis. It gives *you* an opportunity to earn higher commissions than employees on salary are offered, and it gives *them* the opportunity to hire people and pay these employees based solely on their sales ability. It also forces out the ones that are dead wood so to speak—that do nothing for the company, and who would just sit there and expect to collect a paycheck.

What multilevel marketing companies allow people to do is become part of a sales organization on a *part-time* basis, and have the opportunity to see delegation at work. In essence, it opens people's minds to the opportunities and the potential of entrepreneurship, without the risk of a huge financial capital. The money you make is a direct result of the amount of effort you put into the program.

Oftentimes, you'll get a personal coach. This is a person who will train you for free. They are interested in your success, because of the commission structure. If you are making a commission, they are as well. Having someone that you can discuss any type of future goals or direction in your life in a positive way is priceless. It also gives you an opportunity to surround yourself with positive thinking individuals who are setting three to five year goals. Generally, those goals are directed toward results that they will achieve in the company. But the important thing is that they are setting them. Whether you make money or not, being involved with people who are focused on their future, rather than complaining about their past, should jog your mind into doing similar exercises.

Another reason that the legitimate multilevel marketing companies are a promising venture is that they have the potential to broaden your horizon to where you are seeing opportunities that may not be present at your current workaday job. Being part of a sales organization challenges you to go outside your comfort zone and be able to not only sell a product, but be able to sell ideas (or opportunities) to other people.

Finally, and I can't stress the importance of this enough, you will also learn how to *sell yourself.* Learning how to sell yourself is crucial no matter what type of business or opportunity you are pursuing. Even if you do not wish to continue in anything that has to do with sales, *networking* will be something that you have to do in almost any endeavor these days in order to succeed. You'll need to be able to sell yourself and your ideas to anybody, including people that you want to work for you (attorneys, accountants and independent contractors), or to back you (banks, investment companies and other financial loaners).

Some of these companies are publicly traded on the stock exchange and have been around for decades. That is always a good sign. Although the lucrative possibilities have changed over time with world events, economy and changing opportunities coming available in other industries, the lessons that you can get from these programs is again, priceless.

MLM vs. Pyramid Schemes

Now I'm going to discuss the other side of the coin—companies that are interested in one thing and one thing only: putting your money in their pocket. Have you been told that multilevel marketing (MLM) and pyramid schemes are one and the same? Believe me, they are not. There are many *legitimate* MLM companies. However, some companies *claiming* to be "MLM" plans *are* nothing more than pyramid schemes. And pyramid schemes definitely are not legal.

MLM is a way of selling goods or services through distributors (people who are selling the company's product or service on a commissioned basis). These plans usually promise that if you sign up a distributor, you will be paid a commission on your sales, as well as the sales of the people you recruit. This can go on for several distribution levels. However, you DO NOT receive a commission on the distributor fees (the money a person pays to join the program—a.k.a., membership fees) for those people that you recruit. You're only paid on sales of products or services.

Pyramid schemes have a different focus. They concentrate on commissions you earn just for recruiting new distributors, and generally ignore the marketing and selling of products or services. If you're told you'll get a commission on the fee to join, *beware!* Very likely it's a pyramid scheme.

Most states outlaw pyramid business structures. The reason? Plans that pay commissions strictly for recruiting new distributors collapse when new distributors can no longer be recruited. When it collapses, the people in the plan lose money, except for those at the very top. Later, I will cover some other money making programs that are deceitful in nature, do not work and what you can do to prevent yourself from getting trapped by them.

The Federal Trade Commission (FTC) also offers these tips to help you avoid losing money in an illegal pyramid:

- Avoid any plan that offers commissions for recruiting additional distributors without sales of a product or service.

- Beware of plans that make distributors spend money on high-priced inventory.

- Be cautious of plans that claim you'll make money through continued growth of your "downline" as opposed to the sales you make yourself.

- Beware of plans that promise huge earnings or claim to sell miracle products. Just because the promoter makes a claim does not make it true! Ask for hard evidence to back up the claims.

- Beware of shills: "decoy" references that the promoter pays for testimonials to describe fictional earnings.

- Don't pay membership fees or sign any contracts in an "opportunity meeting" or any other high-pressure situation. Take your time and check it out with an attorney, accountant or business consultant before you join.

- Do your homework! Check with the Better Business Bureau and your State Attorney General about any plan you're considering, especially if claims about potential earnings seem too good to be true.

source: Federal Trade Commission

A Closer Look at Pyramid Schemes

Sometimes, pyramids are started and run by honest people who are truly trying to help people make money. However, that does not take away from the fact that they are illegal in almost every state, and cannot work as promised for all of the participants because of a mathematical impossibility. There are not enough people to perpetuate them.

A pyramid scheme, according to the Federal Trade Commission, and the State Attorney Generals of New York and California (among others) is a fraudulent system of making money based on recruiting an ever-increasing number of "investors" or participants. The initial promoters recruit these investors, who in turn recruit more investors, and so on. The organization builds exponentially with an ever-increasing number of people being added to each level, hence the word "pyramid." Pyramid schemes may or may not involve the sale of products or distributorships. Many involve a product or service in order to appear legal. However, it does not matter. The bottom line is, in all pyramid schemes, the only way to make money is by recruiting new members or investors, and not by selling products.

Don't let people promoting pyramids fool you into thinking they are multi-level marketing programs. MLM is a method of selling *products*, directly to *consumers*, without traditional retail stores. The money is made by *selling the products*, and not from recruiting new distributors. In the next chapter, I will cover how to select the right marketing company to work with.

11

Eleven—How to Select the Right Company

I have until now seeded you with practical advice that you can take with you and apply no mater what you decide to do. This chapter is included because, even after people have read my book or seen my lectures, they still ask, "What can I do? I don't have any money? What business can I start?" My suggestion is that you first look at all the industries out there that interest you. Then ask yourself, "Do I feel like starting a business from scratch?" If not, this may be your best alternative: to choose a company to hire on and work with.

So, let's say you decide to work with an established company instead of being self-employed. This may be a manufacturer that you have independently contracted with to sell for them. It could be a marketing company that you become an independent representative for-as in the case of network marketing multilevel companies. Or it could be any other variances on the relationships that you may have with another company. This course of action will give you the advantage of not having to shell out so much of your time and money that it would normally require to start such a business from the ground up and on your own.

This chapter is not intended to convince you that working with preexisting companies is the greatest opportunity on earth. It is designed for (A) those who are already able to see past the prejudice surrounding direct sales and/or network marketing; (B) realize the potential of this form of business; (C) and want to know how to choose the right one for you. If your heart is set on having your own business, then please skip this chapter. However, the questions that I ask herein may help you in your own business as well, whatever that business maybe. In other words, it could help your to "work smarter not harder."

Doing Your Due Diligence

The key to selecting the right company is "doing your due diligence." This is a popular phrase that has caught on in the last few years as people have started to realize that not all companies are created equal. People are beginning to understand that the smart way to select the best business venture for oneself is to thoroughly scrutinize a company before getting involved.

I'm so confused! Everyone claims to be the best. Who can I trust?

There are so many voices out there, it is hard to know who to trust. So, don't just take their information at face value. Don't believe something simply because it is in print. Learn to verify, quantify, and validate information. You need to stop listening to hype and learn to do your own research. Once you have all of the facts, study then play them out in your own mind, and then trust your own intuition. You're the only person who doesn't have a hidden agenda and you're intelligent enough to find and research the facts, and then make your own informed business decisions.

The Criteria for Selecting A Company

Rather than simply running through the criteria I've used for selecting the best company, I've decided to walk you step-by-step through the evaluation process. It will be valuable for you to understand the importance of each criterion. You can use this system to rate any business venture. Listed below are the main criteria I will cover. While you are reviewing these criteria, ask yourself the following questions associated with each criterion:

1. Product Industry:	Which product or service am I going to represent and why?
2. Timing:	Is the timing right? (e.g., Is their product or service going to be a mainstay—or is it transitory in nature: here today—possibly gone tomorrow?)
3. Compensation Plan:	Will the compensation plan work for you? (e.g., Will you be paid enough money, plus other benefits?)

| 4. Company/Management: | How do I evaluate a company and its management team? |
| 5. Product Integrity: | Things to Watch For in a Company (e.g., Is it a product you would not have an objection to personally own and use?) |

Criteria for Selecting the Product Best Industry

When looking for a "hot" product industry, many distributors feel that any legitimate product will do, as long as it is in high demand. However, in today's competitive market, in order for your company to stay on top you must have more than just a "high demand product." Through years of documented research, the top authorities in the industry have come to an agreement on the following characteristics when choosing a high demand product or service. These characteristics can be found in almost all educational books, trade journals, and newsletters. Experts agree that the product or service must have the following characteristics.

1. Traditional: The product or service cannot be too uncommon. It must be similar to other products on the market. The product or service must have a good track record in the marketplace. Traditional products have mass appeal over a substantial period of time.

2. Unique: Although traditional, the product or service must have a unique twist—something that the competition doesn't have or can't get. A special formulator, an exclusive ingredient, a twist in the formulation, or creative processing can make a product unique. A service, on the other hand, must offer something the competition does not. Services are more difficult to customize. The product or service must also be exclusive to one company only. It cannot be purchased in stores or through other suppliers.

3. Consumable: The product or service must be regularly used up and replaced on a monthly basis (at least). This is one of the most important criteria on the list! Without monthly consumption, it is much more difficult to establish residual income. Distributors are constantly looking for new customers.

4. Emotional: The product or service must induce a positive mental or physical change. Products that help people look and feel better can create an emotional bond between the customer and a specific name-brand product.

5. Valuable: The product or service must be worth the price…and maybe more! Prices must not be set too high or too low for the perceived value of the product.

Also, healthy profit margins are essential in order to finance the company and give incentives to distributors.

6. Timely: The product or service must be in high demand RIGHT NOW. The products must appeal to the masses, especially the "baby boomer" generation. The baby boomer group consists of 76 million Americans born between 1946 and 1964. They are the largest buying force in the history of North America and are accustomed to getting what they ask for.

7. Stable: The product or service <u>must</u> me in high demand LATER. Take a look twenty years into the future. Will the product or service still be in high demand? If the answer is yes, you have a winner. If demand on the product will increase with time, that's even better.

How do I use these seven criteria to select a product or service?

Take a specific product industry and put it to the test. For example, let's say you were interested in marketing electronic burglar alarm systems for the home. How does this product check out with the seven criteria?

Is the Timing Right for the Industry?

Let's say the company that your are researching is a manufacturer of VCRs and is looking for distributors to sell thousands of units across the country. Currently in a world of digital DVDs, cell phones, MP3s and CDs. Could there be a better opportunity that has a better timing than VCRs? What if they are manufacturers of payphones, pagers, vinyl records or 8-track players? Timing is key.

Marketing to The Masses…Giving The People What They Want

One of the biggest mistakes people make when trying to decide what product or service to promote, is to choose this product or service based on the wrong reasons. Therefore, I would like to take you through the following exercise, which will help you to discover these right and wrong reasons for yourself.

Now, pretend that you are selecting a product industry today. As you do this exercise, answer the following questions as if your financial future depended on it. Be sure to choose well, because if you make the wrong choice, your chances for success will be virtually eliminated. By the way, there is only one correct choice.

Question: In choosing your own home business vehicle, your #1 concern should be what?

A. **Marketing products and services that are high tech.**

B. **Marketing products and services that are luxurious.**

C. **Marketing products and services that interest me.**

D. **Marketing products and services that benefit me.**

E. **Marketing products and services that benefit as many people as possible.**

F. **All of the above.**

If you chose letter "E" on your own, you're on the right track. I've heard motivational speaker and millionaire Zig Ziglar say, "If you help enough people get what they want, you'll get what you want." It may be fun and exciting to work with choices A-D but there just isn't any profit in marketing products that do not appeal to the masses. Now don't get me wrong, if you have some or all of the factors in the A-D list working for you, its just that much better for you. However, when choosing a product or service, keep the following cautions in mind.

Common Mistakes People Make

While in the business evaluation process, most people tend to choose a product or service for all of the wrong reasons. Here is some advice on avoiding some of the most common mistakes that people in this situation make.

Don't choose to market stereos, computers, or other gadgets simply because you want to market products that are high tech. You should only consider marketing high tech products if you have done the research and know it is <u>extremely profitable</u>. Emotional and personal reasons for selecting a product or service to market are for people who aren't concerned about profit. Millions of people have expensive hobbies.

For example, I know of a man who had a little boy. He enjoyed nothing better than to build elaborate electronic models and devices with his son…especially model trains. He saw an opportunity to get involved in business with a company, which would not only afford him the extra money to purchase the expensive materials for building the tracks, but it would give him the time-freedom he so desperately needed to spend more hours at home. After investigating many opportunities, the man narrowed his choices down to two programs. By good fortune, one of these programs happened to be an electronics company. They had everything from home and car alarms to home entertainment systems to electronic toy cars, boats, and of course trains!! It might seem that the choice would be a no brainer. However, the man decided to choose the other company. This company manufactured and distributed nutritional supplements and personal care products (pills, potions, and lotions). Although his personal interests revolved around the electronics company, he saw more market potential in the second company.

The result? After five years of diligent effort, the man is now semi-retired with a residual income of 5 figures per month. He now has one of the largest collections of electronic toys and gadgets of anyone in town but more importantly, he has the time-freedom to enjoy building the most elaborate electric train track you have ever seen. As for the electronics company? They went through over 800,000 distributors in five years and then declared bankruptcy.

Don't sacrifice profit to market products that are luxurious. After all, which is the larger, more successful company, Coca-Cola or BMW? Which product costs more? Would it be more profitable to market lots of inexpensive consumables or a few high-ticket, non-consumable luxury items? Don't limit your profit potential by marketing products that interest only you and a few others. You may have a personal interest in bagpipes but it's not likely that too many other people are in the market for one. Find out what most people are in the market for and market that.

Although it is important to have a firm personal testimony of your product or service, don't choose to market a product or service *simply because* you experienced personal benefit from it. Just because you had a beneficial experience doesn't mean others will. Likewise, just because you don't have personal benefits from a specific product or service doesn't mean others won't have benefits. I have run into countless individuals who have chosen their networking vehicle based on the pursuit of their own personal interests without giving a thought to what the masses want and need—and they ended up failing miserably.

I met a woman several years ago who really got me to thinking about other's needs over my own. She was a top distributor in a nutritional program and she proudly pointed out one day that she was earning a high six-figure income by promoting an effective nutritional supplement that she herself did not personally use on a daily basis. You see, this woman was about five-and-a-half feed tall and weighed about 110 pounds. She had to shop young miss sizes in some of her clothes. If she got any slimmer, she would be able to slide under doors without opening them. The product that took her to fame and fortune was an herbal weight management product. Almost everyone she introduced to the product was having results. However, she could not afford to lose any more weight so she stayed away from the stuff. The result? Over 10,000 independent sales distributors in her organization in three years and she still does not take the product regularly. It is important not to get hung up on what works for you. Find out how many others it will work on…that's the real test.

Don't make your decision to market a product or service in the heat of the moment at some hyped up rally. Let your emotions calm down to the point where you can use logic and reason to make your ultimate decision. Timing and trends can change over the years. But if a product or service is truly a winner, do you think you will miss out on some big profits if you don't jump in immediately. Many promoters would like to make you think so. Now don't get me wrong. I'm always game for taking someone up on a really good offer. However, the demand on a specific product or service should be safe for weeks, months, and even years after the circus has left town. Don't let anyone make you feel that if you don't sign up right this minute, you'll miss out on everything. Make sure you have the right company, system, and personal commitment before you sign your life away. Remember that this is marketing, not sales. You'll want to offer products that people want and need; not what you think would be fun and interesting to sell.

When the infamous outlaw XX was asked, "Why do you rob banks?" He answered without hesitation, "because that's where the money is." Your answer, when asked "why did you select THAT product industry should be the same as XX. Of course, the comparison only applies on the surface. After all, unlike XX, you're in this for the long-term benefits of ongoing, month-to-month, year-to-year residual income. Not the short term thrill and "flash in the pan" profits of stealing people's money and then speeding away on your horse, dodging a spray of bullets. That's why selecting the right product industry is so important for "real" success and long term prosperity.

Compensation Plans

Picking the right compensation plan can make the difference between success and failure. It's important to look past the hype and the rumors and concentrate on the facts. Look at all of the plans on the market or by similar companies and then choose the best compensation plan. Most important is that you understand and are comfortable with the plan and the amount that you will make for every sale.

In network marketing there are the six most commonly used pay plans. They are the *Breakaway*, the *Unilevel*, the *Matrix*, the *Two-Up*, the *Binary*, and various "Hybrid" or "Combination" plans. I will not go into the pros and con for these compensation plans, but if you are really interested in the full analysis of such plans, please check out Wave Three—The New Era in Network Marketing by Richard Poe. Again, you must feel comfortable and understand how much you will be paid for your efforts.

Scrutinizing the Company and its Management Team

When selecting a company, these are the most important criteria of all. Here is a simple method for analyzing the company as well as the ownership and management of a company. Retrieve as much information as possible from the following sources:

Company Literature—	Review the company history, founders, management and endorsements.
Trade Publications—	Subscribe to several trade publications that evaluate programs.
Dun & Bradstreet—	Order reports to see that the management team is sound.
Attorney General—	Check with the State A.G.s where the company was founded, where it is located today, and any states were it is doing a high volume of business.
Better Business Bureau—	Call the BBB to see if a lot of complaints are listed with a company. You need to know the main phone line of the company you are investigating.

Dept. of Consumer Affairs—	Check with the DCA in 3 or 4 states where the company is doing business.
Direct Sales Association—	The DSA is a non-profit trade organization that speaks out for direct sales and network marketing. They also have established standards of conduct for direct sales companies that must be followed to be an active member. Call (202) 293–5760 for more information.

Things to Watch For in a Company:

Complaints

When researching a company, check with the previously mentioned regulatory agencies. Most of these agencies simply keep track of complaints. If you're looking for an objective source of information here, you probably won't find it. However, listening to these complaints can be helpful. By the way, even the legitimate companies are going to have some complaints from a few disgruntled distributors. There are countless ways to offend people in modern society. What you don't want to find is frequent litigation, many unresolved complaints, or criminal activity.

Public vs. Private

Researching a public company (a company traded on the stock market) is as simple as pulling a Dun & Bradstreet report through your banker or attorney. These reports usually cost a few hundred dollars and are very reliable. Also, request an annual report from the company itself.

It is more difficult to scrutinize a private company since they do not have to release any financial information. Any information that is released by a private company may or may not be accurate since the supplier does not have any incentive to be 100% accurate and objective. Therefore, it is even more critical with a private company to get to know the backgrounds, personal mission statement and motives of the corporate officers. You must be able to unequivocally answer "yes" when you are asked if you really trust the people who are running the company.

Undercapitalized?

Lack of start-up money is one of the top reasons that companies go out of business. Start-up companies often use profits from today's sales to operate the business, hoping that they can pay distributor commissions out of next month's profits. Soon, products start to back order and commission checks arrive late, or not at all. Most undercapitalized companies can't maintain this juggling act for long and end up filing Chapter 11 Bankruptcy.

Company Income Claims & Sales Team Building Services

There are two types of programs you must avoid at all cost. The first type of program is one that guarantees income. Companies that promise you will make a specific dollar figure are in violation of the law, but usually go out of business long before the law even knows of their existence. The second type of program is one that offers to build a sales team or downlines for you. Don't believe them for a second. These programs usually take your money and build their own downlines, leaving you high and dry months later. Report any of these programs to your local State Attorney Generals office.

Distributor Income Claims

Although not necessarily related to selecting a company, this is a common problem that needs to be addressed. If you plan on being the best you can be, decide now that you will not use income claims and projections to build your business. Avoid a company or anyone who uses income claims in public meetings, advertising, and conversation. Not only is it illegal in many states, but it encourages exaggeration and fabrication, giving the entire industry a bad reputation. And it doesn't matter whether the claims are accurate or not, they can still be illegal.

Medical Claims

FDA and FTC attacks against careless companies are getting more and more frequent. Companies and distributors must be increasingly cautious about the claims they make about health products. Even personal testimonials are under increased scrutiny and censure. All companies planning on sticking around must be proactive in self-regulation and should have an aggressive program in place to stop any improper product (and income) claims. Good management teams will not hesitate to reprimand distributors for making improper medical claims and will even cancel distributorships for repeat offenses. After all, the company can be held liable for claims made by independent distributors.

Companies don't succeed, people do!

When selecting a company, take a long hard look at the founders and co-founders. They will set the standards for company integrity and activity. They will attract distributors that reflect their values. They will establish the "company culture" that will attract like-minded people. Your company must be administered by extremely high caliber individuals who have experience, character, and commitment.

I've selected my company…NOW WHAT?

Now you might be thinking…OK, I have done my due diligence, paid my dues, applied the research in this chapter and I have finally selected my company. My job is done! Right?

Wrong. There are three addition steps you MUST take in order to avoid the FOUR most common reasons for failure. Let's review these reasons briefly to show you what you are up against, and then I'll give you some ideas on how to get around these obstacles. I'll start with the one we've been spending so much time on already.

Q: What are the four reasons for failure in working with a company?

1. **WRONG COMPANY:** When people select the wrong company, they fail for two reasons. First, the person will fail because he/she does not have a good experience with the company. If the person does not get along with the company's management, if the product is ineffective, or if the compensation plan is not fair, the person will most likely leave the company within the first 1–2 years. Second, sometimes the person believes in the company one hundred percent. However, due to poor management, bad finances, ineffective products, or lousy compensation, the company goes out of business leaving the distributor high and dry.

2. **WRONG SUPPORT:** Even when the person finds a great company, it is nearly impossible to build a successful business without a supportive management team who offers training and guidance. Without training and support, new distributors are left to their own devices and will soon fail.

3. **NO SYSTEM:** Most beginners are very excited about getting started. However, even very determined individuals will fail within their first year if they are not working a proven system.

4. **NO COMMITMENT:** It's simply human nature. Most people want to take the easy road. It's hard to find people with the determination to stick to it. Lack of commitment is the number one reason for failure. Without a solid commitment, the best company, support and system can't help you. Commitment is essential for success in any field of endeavor. What does it mean to be committed? It means doing whatever it takes to be successful with no excuses. Before you look for a company, you must ask yourself, "Am I committed to doing whatever it takes to make this work?" Then surround yourself with people who share the same commitment.

Up to You!

Okay—I've given you the goods, now get out there and succeed. You will need to take that next step. It is time to take action! Request specific information about the company you are interested in and then apply the principles outlined in this chapter.

12

Deceptive Moneymaking Offers

If you start searching for prepackaged moneymaking offers you are going to get hit with numerous opportunity offers in the mail from the mail order or direct mail marketing industry. Even if a telemarketer calls you with a program to make money, often they have done so because you have responded to some form of direct mail. Even if you never responded to an ad or direct mail letter, the telemarketer will surely send you a sales letter to back up in writing what they have said over the phone.

Unfortunately, there are some programs out there that are intentionally deceptive in nature. This is due to the fact that since there are thousands of people selling opportunities in the mail, it is difficult for the authorities to regulate them all. Having participated in the direct market industry, I have encountered numerous programs offering opportunities via mail order. Some were good, some not so good. The ones that I would like to share with you in this chapter are the ones that you should *avoid*. These programs have an extremely low setup cost, and usually say, "all you need to do is…" and then you will become rich beyond your wildest dreams.

The Enticing Sales Letter

The sales letter for the program you are thinking of trying sounds so convincing. It tells you how millions of people are waiting for this offer, and that your potential market is limitless. It even gives you a convincing illustration showing you how your little investment of a few dollars can make you hundreds of thousands, or even millions of dollars! "Wow!" you tell yourself, "there it is, right on paper." You think that even if you only get a portion of the people to respond, you will still make a bundle of money!

With any pyramid scheme, mail order moneymaking system, or a chain letter, a little common sense and a simple calculator will quickly show you the truth! Do not believe the "statistics" given to you in the sales letter, they are just a bunch of meaningless numbers. Any market researcher will tell you that statistics can be manipulated in many different ways to show you what the promoters want you to see, and not what is realistically possible.

The truth is that most moneymaking programs are based upon principals that have been around for many years. There is no "secret" or "never seen before" method, only variations of systems that have already been established. Be on the lookout for deceptive offers. Remember, if you do not know *exactly* what it is that you are buying, do not waste your money without investigating further. Legitimate companies are proud of what they offer and will have no problem supplying you with additional information!

Learn to Recognize Legitimate Opportunities in Mail Order!

Advising mail order newcomers to avoid deceptive offers is like telling someone to jump in a lake and avoid getting wet! If you jump in a lake, you will get wet. And, if you enter the crazy world of mail order, you are going to encounter deceptive advertisers sooner or later. While many companies are honest and trustworthy, mail order is full of people who will try to sell or promote anything just to make money for themselves.

So, you wonder, how can one avoid getting taken by unscrupulous mail order promoters? Unfortunately, it is not easy. But, there are certain things to look out for when investigating moneymaking opportunities. First and foremost, if you believe you can get rich overnight without putting forth *real effort*, then you will only be wasting your money. You just as well get ready to be the victim of another deceptive program. However, if you are willing to work hard, work smart, and persevere, there are legitimate opportunities out there for you. Some of these can make you wealthy beyond your wildest dreams. The trick is to try as many different (and legitimate) programs as you can until you find one that works for you. Once you do find a program that works, put all your efforts into making that program successful!

Once you start to investigate mail order opportunities, beware! Try to investigate the integrity of each offer and the people promoting the offer. You should be extremely leery of any offers that employ the following tactics:

The "Blind Offer"—This is where the promoter never tells you exactly what it is they are selling. They only tell you how rich they will make you. This is the oldest trick in the book. Nobody can promise you that you will make a certain amount of money, or that their plan "will definitely work for you." If it is not clear from the ad or sales material exactly what it is you are buying or dealing in, do not waste your money and time.

"Payments To Be Made via Cash Only"—Watch out! They want cash only for a good reason! Checks, credit cards, and money orders all leave a paper trail. Cash leaves no trail! The seller or promoter can take cash, send you garbage, or nothing at all, and there is no way for you to find them if they do not want you to. Also, swindlers often want cash to avoid paying their share of income taxes. One exception to this is where the cash amount is very small, and is designated as "for more information." For example, if someone asks for $5.00 or less to cover the cost of sending you more information, you can feel fairly safe sending it to them—PROVIDING THEY ARE A LEGITIMATE COMPANY. The reason some of these people ask for cash when dealing with small amounts of money is because of the cost of processing checks, as well as the cost to recover on bad checks, is prohibitive for such a small amount. So, you can send petty cash if you want to, but be careful—and never send money to a company that you are not sure you can get in touch with if you need to!

Claims "Program Is Legal" Or Quotes "Postal Titles or Laws"—The program is most likely illegal! These people try to misquote the laws or offer phony testimonials and double talk! Any program that requires the exchanging of name positions on a list, or offers a "cheat proof" program is most likely promoting an illegal chain letter, pyramid scheme, or other shady program. Be leery of "gifting programs," or other programs that require you to send money to one or more people on a list, while your name then moves onto the list. Not only are these programs illegal, they will *never* work as designed.

Does Not Give an Address or Phone Number—The reason is simple. They do not want you to know who they are! While it is common, and perfectly okay for a company to use a P.O. Box, or even withhold a phone number, you want to be sure that you can get in touch with them if you have to. Be sure you are confident that you can reach the promoter if you need to. Otherwise, watch out! Legitimate companies are proud of their programs, and will be willing to let you ask for more information. They make it a point to advise you how to reach them.

Before you sign up for an offer that seems "too good to be true," look for these clues...

DECEPTIVE PROGRAMS/OFFERS

- Not clear as to exactly what it is you are buying

- Often uses high-pressure sales tactics

- Sounds too easy, claims "anyone can do it," or "little or no work involved," or "requires little commitment"

- Claims you can make huge amounts of money in little time using their "Secret Method" or gimmick, which is not revealed in the ad

- Makes wild claims, says little about the product, promises great riches instantly

- Uses trick or confusing headlines and ad copy to hide what it is that they are actually selling

- Claims offer is legal, cites U.S. Postal Title 18 or another legality

- Claims to be a "one-of-a-kind" product, or "available for a limited time only"

- Claims to be a "secret" product or plan

- They will not answer questions or inquiries until an order is placed

- The company is hard to find or get in touch with

- Uses outlandish testimonials claiming success

- A "conditional guarantee" is offered that is purposely written to be confusing

- The company offers one product for quick sales, with no repeat business necessary

The following is a guide for you to use when evaluating mail-order programs or offers in which you may have an interest.

LEGITIMATE PROGRAMS/OFFERS

- Offers a believable product or service, clearly tells you what you are buying

- Does not use high pressure tactics

- The offer sounds workable, takes time and effort, and requires commitment

- Says you can make a "reasonable amount of money" in a reasonable time period

- Is based on a known method, or one that seems workable with serious effort on your part

- Avoids wild claims—clearly explains product benefits

- Does not need to state the legality of the offer—it is clearly legal

- Probably one of many companies offering the product

- The product is available when you request to see it

A Typical Moneymaking Offer Broken Down

Is there any truth at all to these get-rich-quick programs? The answer is YES and NO. There is truth to their claims of outrageous incomes. The problem is that what these offers tell you to do is not the real moneymaking formula. They are making a fortune selling secret plans that claim you can get rich following their simple instructions on how to:

- BUY AND SELL EUROPEAN CARS

- SELL BOOKS THROUGH THE MAIL

- SHOW PEOPLE HOW TO PAY OFF THEIR MORTGAGES EARLY

- BUY AND SELL BONDS

- BUY REAL ESTATE WITH NOTHING DOWN

- SELL SPECIAL PACKAGES

- BET ON HORSES AND WIN

The list goes on and on. There are too many of these offers to list. What is important to know is that they all share something in common. They're selling *information* only—there is no product involved.

One popular and profitable moneymaking offer instructs people to send for a fantastic moneymaking secret that can make you outrageous fortunes overnight. The people who respond to this offer are sent a book. The book describes how to sell books and information through the mail. Not once in their full-page advertisement do they mention that what they are selling is a book on how to start your own business selling books through the mail. Yet that's what you received from them.

In their offer, they refer to what you are going to receive as "a secret" or "our revolutionary plan" or "special material." The question is: why didn't they tell you in their offer that they were selling a book on how to start your own mail order business? After all, the book they send to you teaches you how to get fabulously wealthy selling books through the mail, such as books on subjects like home gardening, sports, financial strategies, health, etc. So, why is there no mention of a book in their offers?

The book explains how to set up your own office, get a business license, place advertisements, maintain a good mental attitude and a few other common business tips. But, in a nutshell, the book instructs you that the way to make your millions is to take out space advertisements and classified ads in magazines and newspapers to sell books.

The advertiser delivered their end of the bargain. It *is* possible for someone to make a fortune selling books. You think it over. Although the book that was sent to you does a good job of motivating you and gives you some important basics on starting and running your own business, you are skeptical about putting in a lot of time, effort and money into selling books. So, you decide it is not for you.

You actually have not given the plan an honest try. Therefore you do not take advantage of the money-back guarantee they offered you. Or, you plan to return the book for a refund, but you just don't seem to get around to finding a box, wrapping it up and writing a letter to return it. Before you know it, the thirty day "trial period" is over and you are stuck with the "secret plan."

Does this sound familiar? If not you will definitely encounter an offer such as this in the near future as you search for ways to start a prepackaged home-based business. Millions of people go through this every year. Whether the plan instructs you to sell books, European cars, government Jeeps or credit secrets, the results are often the same. You get a plan that could make a lot of money, but most reasonable people will not risk attempting them.

Their advertisement brings to mind some new and special secret that will make you rich. Some special process or trick that will make you rich overnight. It doesn't bring to mind selling books through the mail.

So why not simply advertise the book? Why not tell people you can show them how to get rich selling others on selling books? Why not? What kind of offer do you think people are more apt to buy into?

1) An advertisement offering unlimited earning potential with very little investment using a secret plan or materials.

-OR-

2) An advertisement offering a book on "How to start your own business selling books through the mail."

Most people would answer the first advertisement of course. Everyone wants to have their own low investment, high profit business. They are enchanted by the opportunity to cash in on some new miracle, moneymaking formula.

On the other hand, many people don't want to buy and read another book, nor do they want to attempt to sell books through the mail. You are probably not going to get rich overnight selling a book on gardening at home. But it *is* possible that one in a hundred or one in a thousand people might be successful at it. It could happen, and that is how these offers can get away with making such fantastic claims. The Federal Trade Commission would not allow them to blatantly lie.

Just how much money are these offers capable of generating? See for yourself. Go to your local library and ask for the current issue of the Standard Rate and Data book or SRDS. Look in the Opportunity Seekers section. Notice all of the lists available for "income opportunity" products. Carefully look at the lists and find a few that are comprised of people who purchased an income opportunity book or a book on starting a business.

How many names are on those lists? 30,000, 150,000, 450,000? Each name represents a sale. A company that sold a book on how to make a fortune overnight selling good luck widgets, sold income opportunity books to that many people.

What was the average unit of sale, i.e., how much do people pay for the book? Multiply the number of names on the list times the cost of the book and you have the amount generated by just one company.

This is proof of the fortunes that can be made and are being made. Do several more of these companies and then compare. You can see the motivation behind these offers really is *huge profits*. Now you know why these people are so willing to sell their moneymaking secrets. All it takes is one successful advertisement and you can have a small fortune in a short time.

The Chain Letter Broken Down

Let's take a simple chain letter program, which is very similar to a pyramid scheme. A chain letter is a letter or email that that promises riches by sending five people listed on the letter a sum of money. Then you continue the chain by removing one of the individuals' information, place in your information, and mail it out to a group of people. When people receive this new letter with your information, they send money to you and the four other people. Eventually, you will have thousands of people sending you money as this chain letter continues. It sounds like an easy way to make some quick cash.

The sales letter might say that your potential market is 260 million people, which is the population of the United States! Well, right away you know that this is not true because every person in the U.S. is certainly not a candidate to purchase your program! They then give you an example of what you can make with "only a 5% response." Which means if you mail 100 letters you get 5 people to order. Remember what I often point out here, even the very best programs pull a 1–2% response. A 3% response is considered excellent, a 5% response is phenomenal.

I did some research to show you what the realistic "potential market" is for ANY moneymaking program. First of all, as I mentioned, there are approximately 260 million people in the U.S. Of these, approximately 176 million are between the ages of 20–80 years old, the ones who will realistically be able to purchase any program. Of this 176 million, approximately 11%, or 19 million are below the poverty level. These are certainly not good candidates. Another 10%, or 17 million are at an income level far above the norm. These people are not viable candidates either, because they already have all the money they need!

So, we are left with approximately 140 million "potential" customers. Because many of these live in the same household, are married, or for other reasons, we will be generous and say that 50% of them are actually bona fide prospects. We are now left with 70 million. A huge number, but not the 260 million many of these companies tout as the potential market!

Now comes the interesting part. Let's take a typical chain, pyramid, or bogus MLM program, generating payments on five levels, claiming a 5% response, based on each participant mailing out 1,000 programs.

By level 5 you would need more participants than there are people in the entire WORLD, much less the U.S. And, for those of you who say, "But I can still make a lot of money on 4 levels," use your common sense math! Remember, our total realistic potential market is only 70 million! If your program requires

125 million, this means that there are *not enough people to participate!* It is not possible. And, even if you make it to level three, it will still take 2.5 million participants! If all these did in fact participate, only 28 people would even have a *chance* to make this money! That is because after the full program cycled 28 times, the 70 million potential market would be used up!!

You can now see why the mere numbers required to make these programs work are not possible! Next time you are considering a program, do your math! Figure out how many people you must get to respond, and then figure out if it is viable. Chances are it is not. Remember, the 70 million is just an approximate "potential" market.

A legitimate MLM program can work because you are recruiting a downline that will give you *repeat* Business. It is the repeat business that gives you a residual income. But, if the MLM program requires too many participants, it will also fail because the numbers are just not there to support it!

The only people who ever make any money on chain letters, pyramid schemes, or bogus MLM programs are the initial promoters who sell you the mailing lists. Keep in mind not only the impossibility due to the math I have shown you, but also the fact that many of these programs are mailed to the same names!

Chain letters and bogus MLM make up the bulk of the opportunities advertised in the nation's hundreds of independent publications or by direct mail dealers. By contrast, these same offers are not listed along with the national advertising seen in major publications such as *Income Opportunities* or *Entrepreneur.* There are at least two important reasons for this: one, the expense would be prohibitive. And two, the publisher's editorial department would not allow them to appear.

If what you are receiving in your mailbox is an indication of all the money-making activity going on, business clearly is thriving. This also points to our current woeful national economy at a time when fewer and fewer can afford to buy their own home or to make even an acceptable standard of living. So what we are looking at is a massive "underground" attempt to develop wealth by mostly unorthodox means. This has resulted in enticing ads for wealth building, which have become more prevalent than in recent memory and even more blatant. This is "prime time" for *snake oil* salesmanship. The competition is tough as more and more clever salesmen peddle their wares. And this is where they lead the unwary astray.

"Earn $2,000 Weekly Stuffing Envelopes At Home"

It amazes me that this deceptive program is still around. In the late 1970s and early 1980s this type of deceptive program was at its peak, reeling in millions of unsuspecting people. The Postal Inspector clamped down, and it has been severely curtailed. But, it keeps making a comeback, disguised in various forms. Sometimes it is promoted as "envelope stuffing," sometimes as "packaging and mailing our manuals," or "stapling booklets" or some other *creative* variation. I still receive several pieces of mail each week promoting these types of programs. Many of the people promoting them may be honest, but they have just been mislead by the shady companies behind the program.

Why do these kind of programs continue? First of all, the advertisements are very enticing. They usually say something like *"Earn $2.00 for every envelope you stuff! Work At Home! Everything Supplied! Success Guaranteed!"* or *"Earn $15.00 for every booklet you staple."* You tell yourself, "All I have to do is stuff a lot of envelopes, assemble books or staple booklets and I'll get rich!" You get so pumped up that you are ready to write your check for that "good faith" deposit of $30 or more. It is so easy, (something I am always pointing out it *seems*). But, think about it for a second. If a promoter has a legitimate business going for them, why would they need home workers to "stuff" their envelopes or "staple" their booklets? Don't be fooled by them telling you that their staff cannot handle it, or some other implausible excuse. The fact is, they could easily go to a mailing house and have their sales letters machine printed, folded, and inserted into envelopes for pennies each. Why would they want to pay someone $2.00 for something they can have done for pennies? Staple a booklet? Why would ANYONE pay you to do this when a machine can do it instantly, and all day long for about 2¢ per booklet, no matter the size?

The programs come in many variations, but basically here is what you'll receive for your "registration fee":

1. You get a poorly printed instruction sheet or flyer, usually advertising a book or other product.

2. You receive *one* copy of an advertising flyer, which you must get reprinted at your own expense.

3. You are instructed to place an ad in a publication advertising the envelope stuffing or other "secret" get rich plan, asking people to send you a SASE.

This is where you get "all the supplies you need, stamps, envelopes, and customer names."

You "stuff" the envelopes with a copy of the advertising flyer for the book or whatever the promoter is selling. If the customers order, you get a commission of $2.00 or more. If you do not get any orders, you will receive nothing regardless of how many envelopes you are stuffing with the sales flyer. You only get paid if you "stuff" an envelope with an order for the promoter! You will rarely get more than a few orders. The promoters are getting rich from the "registration fee" they charge you.

The sales circulars promoting these deceptive programs are well written and contain a lot of play-on-words. For example, saying that "you will be provided all supplies free of charge" is not an outright lie, but it is certainly deceptive. The only way you are "provided" the supplies is if you advertise for SASEs, have the sales circulars printed, and spend a lot of time mailing the circulars so others will mail you SASEs.

If you ever get any type of flyer telling you that you can get rich stuffing envelopes, packaging manuals, or anything where they claim they need "home workers" to mail out their information, be very skeptical. Odds are it is nothing more than a deceptive program. And, if you cannot call and ask for additional information, NEVER send your money to them! A legitimate company does not need YOU or anyone freelance to stuff their envelopes!

Foreign Lotteries By Mail

First of all, trying to attain financial freedom by lottery is absolutely, positively not the way to go. Lotto fever! With all the hype from State lotteries it's easy to catch. Next thing you know, you receive a brochure in the mail enticing you to play a foreign country's lottery—promising huge payouts if you participate. The brochure makes it sound so easy and possible to win huge because you share in a pool of lottery tickets. You get all excited, and figure this will increase your chances of winning a fortune and decide to send in your check. STOP! If you're thinking of playing a foreign lottery, the U.S. Postal Inspection Service has some advice for you—***don't do it!*** Why not? Because:

• It's illegal. A federal statute prohibits mailing payments to purchase any ticket, share or chance in a foreign lottery.

- It's impractical. Unlike playing your state's lottery, you cannot be certain you will receive any winnings and there is no way to retrieve your money. What are you going to do, fly to Europe and try to hunt them down and collect?

- Chances are it's not a lottery at all, just a deceptive program to get your money. Since they operate outside the U.S., it is next to impossible to enforce the laws.

Most lottery solicitations sent to addresses in the U.S. do NOT come from legitimate foreign lottery sources. Instead, they come from "bootleggers" who seek huge fees from those wishing to play. Typically, if you play, you'll never see any tickets issued by the foreign government-operated lottery you supposedly entered. The bootleggers issue bogus "confirmations of entry" and simply take your money!

Generally, it is illegal to send ANY lottery material through the mail. This includes, among other things, letters or circulars concerning lotteries, tickets or any paper claiming to represent tickets, chances or shares in a lottery, and payments to purchase any such tickets, chances or shares. Congress has made some exceptions, but only for STATE lotteries mailed to people WITHIN THAT STATE!

Also beware of bogus lotteries which are operated in the U.S. by individuals or companies not affiliated with the government. These are ALL illegal. One we received recently was from "The People's Lottery" with a P.O. box for their address. Their ploy was to ask people to send three payments of $5.00 (cash, of course) to receive two lucky "lottery numbers." You'd then receive a circular so you can get all of your friends involved. They even went so far as to claim that *"you don't need to know how this works, as long as it is legal and works for you, that is all you need to know. We guarantee it."* Right! This is nothing more than a disguised chain letter and as such is ILLEGAL and IMPOSSIBLE to work!

If you receive a mailed lottery solicitation that you think may be illegal, turn the entire mail piece over to your local postmaster or the nearest Postal Inspector.

"Get One Million People To Send You $2.00"

Perhaps you have seen this ad or received a circular for the program, or one similar to it. The ad reads "How To Get One Million People To Send You $2.00. Learn my easy method! Plus receive proof this method works!" Well, we knew exactly what this method was, and what the "proof" was that we were going to receive. We rushed off our $2.00 entry fee.

Did we receive some earth-shattering secret program? Some special key to unlocking financial freedom that nobody else had? Did we receive even $2.00 worth of information? The answer to all of the above is a resounding NO! We only received a circular, which was simply a blow up of the ad. We also received the "proof," along with a sample ad to place, and a list of companies that would print and mail camera-ready ads for $2.00 per inch.

And, what was the "proof" that the system works? You guessed it! The circular proclaiming *"Here Is The Absolute Proof!!! You Responded, You Ordered."*

While this program may or may not be illegal, unarguably, it is deceitful. First of all, while it is *possible* to get a million people to respond to your ad or circular, it is not *likely*. For example, if you do the math (remember that?) at an improbable 1% response to your ad, you would have to get your ad in front of 100 million potential prospects to get your one million responses! This is just not realistic!! Also, this program is unethical for other reasons. You are not getting anything in return, except the deceitful advice to go ahead and place the same ad to dupe others! Finally, this is certainly not going to build you a mail order business. The key to mail order success is *repeat business.* Once you sell this program to a customer, do you really think you will ever be able to sell them anything else in the future? NO WAY! They will know that you are not a legitimate mail order operator, and that you do not sell programs of substance.

Another way to judge a program, as well as the person and/or company selling it, is by the quality of the materials you receive. For example, if this program worked as advertised, the entity we purchased it from should be rich, right? In any event, they should be able to supply high quality printed materials. We received very poor quality photocopies, which were not even close to camera ready. And this company is going to show YOU how to make 2 million bucks? Don't count on it! This is just another deceptive program that should be avoided.

Be A Millionaire In One Month GUARANTEED!

NO legitimate program can guarantee you that you will make a dime, much less a *million dollars!* Period.

What To Do If You Feel You've Been Taken in a Deceptive Program

If you've been taken by one of these program, there are a few things you should do. First of all, contact the company for a refund. If they refuse, or give you the run-around, contact the postmaster in the area that the company is located (NOT where you are located) and send them documentation of why you feel you were ripped off. Next, contact the State Attorney General in the state that the company operates and file a complaint. Next, contact the Better Business Bureau and file a complaint. For a listing of all BBB offices, visit their web site at: **www.bbb.org.** You'll find a lot of beneficial information at this site. Some other useful organizations to contact are:

- Department Of Consumer Affairs—800-952-5210

- National Consumers League (NCL)—800-876-7060

- Federal Trade Commission—Washington, D.C. 20580

The above are also valuable sources of information regarding direct marketing laws and regulations, as well as potentially deceptive programs. Don't allow yourself to get ripped off! There are numerous resources available to help you!

Please Be Realistic

Let's say you had never repaired a car engine before and you decided to overhaul your car's engine. You go out and buy a manual from an expert in the field and you read it cover to cover. You would expect to spend some money on tools and supplies. You wouldn't expect because you read this manual once to just go right out and immediately get the engine overhauled perfectly in record time. You would expect to make a few mistakes but use the manual as a guide—you'd learn as you go.

Here's another one: Let's say you decide to lose 20 pounds. You read a great book on weight loss. You realize you'll need to exercise and change the way you eat. You haven't exercised in 20 years. Would you go out and run two miles as hard as you could and then get on the scale and expect to see 20 pounds gone?

I recite these two examples because for some reason, when it comes to acquiring wealth, some people just throw their common sense out the window.

Now I realize there are some sleazy operations in this market, but there are in every market. My point here is that a lot of people I've spoken to have completely unrealistic expectations and then, of course, they feel "ripped-off" when money doesn't pour out of the sky after they order something.

Starting a home-based business is, in my opinion, the easiest and quickest *legal* way I know of to make money. The start-up costs are very small and the potential for quick profits are amazing—within reason! It is *still* a business and requires time and effort. For someone who has never done it before, it will require a learning period and some trial and error much, much less than most other businesses I know of, but it is still a requirement just the same.

I have a lot of compassion for people, especially ones that have been 'taken' by the con men. But, I also realize that until an individual truly takes responsibility for their own direction in life, they will always be the victim of someone or something. When a person truly takes that power (which they have all the time) they begin to see things differently and begin to truly create a life.

13

Taking Control of Your Cash Flow

What Are the Keys to Controlling Cash Flow?

I've discussed what you need to do to not only to have an idea for a business, but to also focus on your goals and manage your time. If you choose not to start a business from scratch and are looking at some prepackaged business opportunity, I have explained how some of them actually do work and which ones to avoid. But those skills by themselves aren't enough to guarantee you success. You can have achievable goals and determination, but unless you are in control of your cash flow, your business can and probably will fail.

In this session, you'll find out what you need to do to control your cash flow. It is mainly geared to those who have started a small business on the side, whether it is a your own home-based business or you are distributing a product or service for another company. Whatever the case may be, this section is for the people who have already started to generate revenue with their business, whether it is just a couple hundred dollars for the very first time or even if you are making over $10,000 a month. These will be questions that you need definitive answers to, otherwise your business may trap you in an ever downward spiral: How do you manage your money? What should you do with your profits? How can you be sure you're being realistic about how much money you're making? What are the basic fundamentals you need to know about business? And how can you keep from making mistakes?

I'll give you the answers to these questions, but before I do that, there's a very practical question you might have to answer for yourself.

Is This Your Hobby or Your Business?

First off, if you treat a business opportunity as a hobby, your chances of success are minimal at best. By their very nature, hobbies are seldom "for profit" endeavors. There are a few exceptions, but by and large, the money that goes into a hobby is a one-way stream.

Here's a story that can help you be sure you're serious about your business and not just indulging a hobby. I know a woman who started a business selling cute little children's dresses for girls between two and six years old. She figured this would be an ideal business, because she had done this before as a hobby. So far, so good, because she decided to go with something she knew and liked. So she bought a few dresses from a local manufacturer, and she sold them to her neighbors. It was fun and she got very excited because she made a little profit right away.

Then she went to a couple of different manufacturers and ended up on a shopping spree buying these little dresses. She loved shopping, and she was happy as she remembered when her own little girl used to look so cute in these dresses. But now that she had so much inventory, she needed to do more than go to her neighbors to sell them. Suddenly, it was time to go to swap meets, advertise her merchandise, and even go door-to-door outside her neighborhood. It wasn't as much fun as it was the first time because she wasn't in her comfort zone any longer. She had to do more than just shop and show her purchases off to her friends.

This was the point when the woman had to ask herself a hard question: Was this her hobby or was it her business? It's important to have an interest in and enjoy the business you start, but the key is to know the difference between your business and your hobby. If this is a question you think you need to ask yourself, do it right away, before you find yourself in a business you weren't prepared for.

How Do You Manage Your Money?

Whatever you choose as your business, it can all fall apart if you don't know how to manage your money. When you are trying to build a home-based business, you're beginning something new, and that's exciting. But I see a lot of people who start out by spending an enormous amount of money on excessive inventory or unnecessary items just to make them feel like they are in business. They spend money on things they don't need. When you're working out of your home, there are some obvious tools and supplies that you'll need to get, such as business cards, stationery, a separate telephone line, and a fax machine. But I have seen people who have made their first sale then go out and buy themselves a new car. It's good to *think* big in certain instances, because it can put you in the mindset that failure is not an option. But *spending* big is not a good idea when you are dealing with a variety of unknowns.

How Do You Effectively Reinvest Profits?

Suppose you decide to work for a multilevel financial services company. Let's say you are selling life insurance and mutual funds on commission-based pay, and your first month generates $400 in profit. It's exciting when you make your first money in your home-based business. But what are you going to do with that money?

I've seen people take that $400 and reward themselves with nice dinners out or even a trip to Vegas. They rationalize that they are rewarding themselves for their hard work. Reward can be a good form of motivation. But don't you think there might be something better to do with that money you earned through your business to make sure you *stay* in business? What I did with my first $400 was to put it back into the business and let the money ride. This is the best way to get real rewards.

When I began my home-based business, I didn't have very much money. I started my last company with no more than $200—and a lot of sweat and hard work. When that $200 brought back $600 in revenue, I repaid myself the $200 and I reinvested $400 back into the business. That $400 returned $1,200 in revenue—but this time it was all profit. I didn't take anything out of that $1,200, because I'd already repaid my initial investment. I took the whole amount and rolled it back into the business, and it roughly tripled in revenue. I repeated this over and over again until before I knew it, I was generating over $200,000 a month. And I reinvested $100,000 a month of that from then on.

The best way to make money and make your business grow is to reinvest as large a portion of your earnings as you can back into your business. When you make your first $5,000 or $10,000, you may not feel comfortable putting as much as I did back into your business, but do you see my point? If I had rewarded myself right away with that first $400, I could never have achieved the revenue I did. I created and followed a plan and I stuck to it, calculating and minimizing my risks. Wouldn't you rather see your investment increase tenfold and beyond instead of rewarding yourself and showing off with a lavish party? I was able to reward myself along the way, but what I did was to allow my business to flourish first. Let me give you an example:

One way of selling your product or your service is by placing ads in newspaper or magazine classifieds. Let's say the first ad you take out costs $100 and you make $400 from it. Reinvest in your business by repaying yourself the $100 and taking out a $300 ad. If the $300 ad nets $800, reinvest as much of that as you can and then try taking out several ads in different magazines or newspapers. If you work your way up bit by bit, there is little risk. Doing it this way, you'll learn what the most profitable ad sizes and advertising sources are.

By reinvesting your profits, you can safely test advertising sources and methods and only keep using the ones that work. You repaid you initial investment, so you aren't risking anything. Using this method, you are seeing the big picture that will make your business succeed and grow.

Rolling your profits back into your business instead of taking an instant reward means that you are playing with nothing to lose. After you see how your business can succeed, that's the time to stand back, take a look at your revenue, decide how much to keep reinvesting into the business, see if you want to expand, and give yourself some of the profit as a reward. And that's great, because isn't it important to have fun when your hard work has been successful? Of course it is. But remember that nothing can kill a would-be profitable home-based business faster than not understanding the difference between earnings and profit.

Still, when you make a profit, spending too much too soon can also jeopardize your business. Let me give you an example. I know someone who worked for a shipping company for 13 years. But he wanted to have his own home-based business, so he joined a multilevel marketing company in the financial services industry. He kept his job with the shipping company and he worked four hours a day at his home-based business. After a year, he became a $100,000 earner. This means that $100,000 was reported on his 1099.

Encouraged by his success, he and his wife decided that working at home for this multilevel company was what they were destined to do. He quit his job at the shipping company and concentrated on his own business. This would have been wonderful except for one thing: He and his wife immediately went out and bought a $120,000 Mercedes. And this was after only one year of making a decent income. But they wanted to show the world their success. It turned out to be too soon to make a move like that. And over the next several months they struggled to meet the car payment each and every month.

Unfortunately, I've seen other people who reward themselves too quickly at the beginning and end up losing the potential to let their profits ride and reinvest them. They may make $3,000 to $5,000 a month in their home business, but they will never go beyond that because they end up spending all of it for living and entertainment. Making that much money is a great start, but since they spend everything they make, they will always have a small business and it won't be that much different than having a salaried job.

Are You Deluding Yourself About Your Wealth?

As your business begins to make a profit, make sure not to delude yourself by thinking that your revenue is the actual amount of money you are making. Some people make $100,000 in revenue from their home-based business in the first year or two, and that's an accomplishment they can be proud of. The mistake they make is that they start telling themselves and others that they make six figures. They aren't keeping in mind that even though they made $100,000 in revenue, it cost them $65,000 to run their business. So in reality they make less than six figures—much less than six figures. They have really only made $35,000 (approximately $3,000 a month), but they seriously believe they're making an average of $8,300 a month.

Because they have deluded themselves about how much they make, they start spending $6,000, $7,000, or $8,000 a month. They tell themselves, "I make six figures, so I deserve to reward myself." These are people who cannot discipline themselves. Even though they have been successful in what they've done so far, they don't understand that their current success is just a stepping-stone to real success. By not being realistic, they are risking their business and their future.

Therefore, as larger amounts of money start to come in, remember that this money is *revenue* and not profit. Do not fall into the trap that many people who have made a lot of money have quickly fallen into. You must avoid getting caught up in the hype, because this becomes the instant killer for your success. You need to remember what you have learned about focus and goals in this program.

Furthermore, you need to keep accurate records of your expenses and do a tally at the end of each *month*—not just at the end of the year for tax purposes. You need to see *on paper* your actual *profit* and live your lifestyle based on *that* figure. But in doing so, always keep in mind what I said earlier about reinvesting some of your profit back into your business. That will insure that you'll continue to live in the manner to which you've become accustomed.

How Do You Give Yourself a Reality Check?

When the money starts rolling in, are you going to rush out and rent an office in a fancy building? That big rent payment could kill you if you exhaust the market for your product or service and need to start over with a new one. You have to ask yourself these questions about your business: Is my product seasonal? Will there be slow periods when not as much money will be coming in? Will I still have extra money available for when I really need it? Do I really need a cell phone or a new car for my business? Step back and look at your business realistically. This way, you'll keep from falling into the "reward trap" before your business is really successful and able to sustain itself—even in periods of weak economy.

Can you distinguish between accomplishment and hype? You're going to need to give yourself a reality check on a regular basis. Some sales organizations need you to be excited and motivated about their company constantly. They'll tell you how great you're doing, whether or not it's true, just to keep you excited. But no matter how great that motivation and excitement feels, when it comes down to reality, understanding how to read your own financial situation—your own profits and losses for the year—is crucial. This is the only way you can reward yourself for your real accomplishments and not your hype.

How did you *really* do this year? How much money did you *net* last year? How much money did you end up *keeping* out of what you made last year? Are you sure you're in a better financial position than you were the same time last year? Or the year before? These are all questions that you need to ask yourself. If you haven't made money with that company after five years, isn't all that excitement pretty worthless?

You can find help in answering these "reality check" questions from an accountant. As I said before, you should seek out mentors. The right financial advisor needs to be someone who can help you keep your goals in sight. You don't need a salesperson who is trying to sell you insurance or investments. You need someone who can clearly illustrate for you how much money you are really making. An accountant or other financial mentor can make sure you understand the difference between revenue and profit. You need to know how the money you earn from your home-based business differs from those W-2 earnings you got from an employer. Then you need to shift—or adjust—your business methods accordingly. It is impractical to keep doing the same thing if the same thing is keeping you at the same place. Stay with it only if you can prove, on paper, steady growth.

What Are the Basic Rules of Business?

Now that you are in business for yourself, you want to do things right and give your new business every chance for success. If you're going to use newspaper and magazine ads to market your product or service, don't spend a lot of money until you've done research, testing, and planning. Research and planning are essential to the success of any good business. If you jump right into a full-page advertisement in a national magazine without test-marketing your product or offer, you may lose a lot of money unnecessarily.

- *Start small*—Test your product before buying expensive advertising space. Remember how I told you to reinvest your profits from one ad into larger or multiple ads? The first, small ads let you promote your product and gauge the response. This is your acid test for your product or service. This lets you know whether or not you're onto something that is going to sell easily and to a wide demographic—or is going to require extra effort on your part to locate a niche market.

- *Test realistically*—If you have a large-scale idea, you may want to go to your local college and ask a business professor if he can have his students help you with market research. They could end up being a valuable source of new ideas for marketing and/or improving your product, and it won't cost you that much. If you have the money and think your product needs it, you can go to a professional business consultant and retain their services for market research and testing. Hundreds of businesses fail each year because of poor financial planning and lack of testing. Too many people get all excited and want to jump right into the deep end. Before they know it, all of their seed money has been exhausted on expensive whims.

- *Cover all of your bases*—If you decide to advertise your product in national magazines, find publications that already have offers similar to yours in them. Once you have found a few that seem like good prospects, place small ads in two or more of them. Be sure to key your ads so that you will know which ad in which periodicals are producing the most replies. Then go for larger ads in the magazines that worked the best. Don't spend all of your advertising dollars on one big ad until you're sure it can bring in good revenue.

- *Don't get buried with inventory*—The FTC (Federal Trade Commission) requires that you have a product on hand before you advertise it for sale. Also most advertisers will want a sample of your product before they run your advertisement, to prevent people from advertising things they can't supply.

But nothing says you have to have a thousand samples on hand. Don't stock up heavily until the orders start coming in.

- *Keep simple and easy-to-understand records*—General business bookkeeping ledgers are available from most office supply stores or you can buy some simple computer software. Start out immediately with proper bookkeeping, and discipline yourself to keep it up. If you put off record keeping, you may not remember everything you have done or exactly where your expense money is going. Bookkeeping is also very important for tax purposes. If you have a problem with the IRS they will want to see your bookkeeping. If it is clean, clear and precise, you will save yourself innumerable headaches.

- *Plan for taxes*—Many things are deductible when you own your own business. But you need to keep receipts for everything that you plan to deduct in case you are audited. A good tax preparer can tell you which expenses are deductible as well as how much of your earnings you need to set aside for income tax.

- *Discipline yourself*—If your new business is going to be your sole source of income, be sure not to get too comfortable with being your own boss. When you are working for yourself, especially when you work at home, it's easy to develop some bad habits. Set regular work hours for yourself, like 8 to 4 or 9 to 5. But make sure these hours are strictly for work. Don't let yourself fall into the habit of doing housework or other chores during work hours. Stay focused on your work. Discipline will be a key factor in making your business successful.

How Can You Learn From Others' Mistakes?

Tenacity is a wonderful word. Tenacity—just plain not giving up—is essential for your home-based business. The stakes are just too high! Almost all successes are built upon the ruins of earlier failures, and you can be sure that one wealth-building advertiser after another (all now millionaires) learned from their mistakes. Almost all of the mistakes that have sabotaged home-based businesses were the result of not heeding one or more of the fundamental business principles I covered in this section. I strongly advise you to reread this section, make notes, and be sure you have a clear understanding, which will give you a sound foundation to operate from. This way, your path to success can be straight and true, and you'll be the one in control. By following my proven methods and doing everything "by the book," you'll shorten the trial and error period—and shorten the time until you are able to make good money from your business.

14

What To Do After You Finish Reading This Program?

This is the most crucial part of any program. The thing that happens time and again, is most people get extremely motivated as they start reading through a program like this, but few people actually finish it. And of those that do finish, there are only a few of them who will actually use the information. How are YOU going to apply this information? Most people will be very excited, yet they do not know what to do next. As they were going through the program, everything made sense to them. We connected. But then you tend to see some of the poor business habits that mold some people's future. So you're all excited and you now have the information and you know how important it is for you to take action and follow through, and you're ready to apply this in your life. But tomorrow happens. And you do not know what to do next.

This section covers what you will need to do *starting today* in order to get the most benefit out of this program—and not become one of those people who took down very good notes, yet tomorrow they will do absolutely nothing.

So where do you stand? Was this program just useful information that you have on hand? Or will this information be something you can start applying *today* and it becomes part of your *daily life*? Will it be information that if you were to begin applying today, it would mean that of all of the goals that you had set for yourself in the Focus and Goals session of this program will come to pass?

First things first. A few of you have not done your Focus and Goals session of this program. You absolutely need to do that right now. If you skimmed over that, or planned to come back to it after you finished the book, you need to do it NOW. Please sit down in a quiet room with blank piece of paper and a pen, and complete the exercise.

If you have completed that portion of the program where you have written down your financial goals for the first 1, 3, and 5 years, you are well ahead of the game. However, like I explained in that section, the exercise will do you absolutely no good if that goal sheet is stuck in a folder, in some book, or underneath a stack of papers on your desk, where you'll never see it again. That piece of paper absolutely needs to be on a wall (such as the bathroom, next to the mirror) where you will see it at least once every 24 hours. What you need to do right now is go find that piece of paper and Scotch tape it up in a prominent place.

With that done, starting right now, make and begin your *Six Things* list that you need to do today (see Session 7). And please, complete one task before you move on to the next. If you do not have all *Six Things* that you can think of, four or five is also okay, because the main goal is to have your *Six Things written* on a piece of paper and not inside your head. This frees up your mind for innovation. And, as things come up throughout the day just write those down. But remember do not jump onto another project, unless you are making a conscious decision while looking at your list, that you are going to stop pursuing the current project, the one that you were working on, and you are now moving on to the priority project. Also make sure that at least one of the *Six Things* are completing or moving to complete one of your 1–5 year goals. In three months, you need to see if you are moving toward or away from your Focus and Goals sheet pasted up on your bathroom wall.

The third thing that you need to do, starting today, is to make sure that the technology in your life is working to your advantage. Eliminate the technology that is stealing time away from you. Have the technology that is available to you making you more efficient. Tonight, sign up for automatic bill pay. An average person may have between 7 to 10 bills that they need to pay on a monthly basis. Whether it is your school loan, credit card payment, car payment, rent, or anything else, have them automatically deducted from your checking account. This will decrease your wasted time and virtually eliminate this portion of non-productivity.

Go over the check list that is provided with this program. That check list will help guide you through this program. It takes all the information that was provided in this program and consolidates it down to simple notes to follow. Make sure to complete the checklist by placing in the date that the task has been completed and a check mark right next to it. As long as you are doing this you will be able to make sure that you are on track at all times.

Read through this program over and over. I would say a minimum of five times. I cannot stress that enough. Information like this needs to be reinforced—especially if you're not surrounded by people who think this way. This information should be ingrained in your mind to help you discover new opportunities as you are encountering your daily life and activities. Do your best to get tapes, books or other material by some of the people that I encouraged you to listen to or read up on.

Check	Date	Activity
[ ]	_____	Read Chapters 1–12
[ ]	_____	Stopped listening to negative people
[ ]	_____	Found a Mentor or Purchased Tape of Mentor
[ ]	_____	Started a business
[ ]	_____	Completed Focus & Goals Exercise
[ ]	_____	Signed and placed Focus & Goal Worksheet on wall
[ ]	_____	Started Six Things
[ ]	_____	Started to Delegate (Example: Automatic bill pay)
[ ]	_____	Started to reinvest _____% of your profits
[ ]	_____	Reviewed Chapters_____
[ ]	_____	Reviewed Chapters_____
[ ]	_____	Reviewed Chapters_____
[ ]	_____	Reviewed Chapters_____
[ ]	_____	Reviewed Chapters_____
[ ]	_____	Reviewed Chapters_____
[ ]	_____	Reviewed Chapters_____
[ ]	_____	Reviewed Chapters_____
[ ]	_____	Reviewed Chapters_____

If you have not done so already, start a business—any business. Or if you don't know what kind, I would suggest that you join a multilevel marketing program in your local area. If you are in an inside sales position, I would suggest you go to an outside sales position where you are mentored by goal-oriented, success-oriented or money-motivated people. They will gladly teach you how to "sell yourself." My suggestion is that at first you do not get absorbed into their program as an employee—rather as an *intern* so that you are there to learn something. That way the organization will teach you delegation and focus and goals. You'll learn how to set and achieve goals and you'll learn how to leverage yourself by working with other people. Your choice to continue with their program full time will then be a decision that you'll be in a well-educated position to make. This country allows opportunities like this (interning) to exist so take advantage of them.

Remember to *learn* all you can at your current job. You can always learn something no matter how limited you think the opportunities are. When I was at Kinko's and was working for my sales manager, I was building a side marketing business. This side business was not conflicting with my work and I was doing well with it. After awhile, my side business flourished to the point that it was paying me nearly six times as much as what I was earning at Kinko's. Also, I was earning significantly more than my sales manager. However, his knowledge of how to manage professional salespeople, his organizational skills, as well as how to communicate with Fortune 500 companies, was the type of information that I needed—regardless of the income that I made over him. So I decided to stay on there, learning and growing in invaluable business knowledge. It was one of the best decisions that I made, to continue to learn from a top-notch sales and marketing organization.

My Interpretation of These Programs

In regards to programs like this book and others I've mentioned regarding personal development on focus and goal setting, I compare them to a "genie in a lamp." They allow you to basically "make a wish" and have your wish come true. That is my quick definition of these programs. You need to understand that randomly shooting for your success is just not going to make it happen. You need to know where you are right now, where you want to go, be able to take specific actions and follow through—as well as being able to see if it's working and make slight adjustments. After I have read or listened to these programs, sometimes ten or more times, they become a part of me and made my wishes come true. Obviously, you know that they were not actually *wishes*, but were *goals* that I had set in my life. They were directions that I wanted to go toward, and evolve as a person.

So let this become your new journey. If you have gotten this far in the program, I hope that this is not the first time you are reading my words. Hopefully, this is your second, third or even fifth time you have let me say this to you. As you should know, luck has little to do with getting what you want. Nor does wishful thinking. However if you've really absorbed the information within this program and applied it to your career goals, I say to you, "good luck and best wishes! And to add to that, I wish you skill, perseverance and ultimate success to the highest degree that you are capable! May you use this new knowledge to make your first million!"

About the Author

Ken Hayashi, was born and raised in Southern California. He is a fourth-generation Japanese-American who by age 17 was producing numerous live shows airing on ESPN and E! Television and segment-produced two Emmy Award Shows. After studying abroad in Oxford, England he began working with several marketing organizations and generated several million dollars in sales by age 26, then "retired." In fact, he has been "employed" (not counting "self") only eight months in his life. An accomplished lecturer and trainer with numerous awards and recognition in sales and marketing, he has been featured on Fox TV and in the Wall Street Journal, and he continues to lecture at universities and high schools. He currently lives in San Diego with his wife, Somruthai, and three daughters, Alexis, Ashley and Natalie as a full-time husband and father. Visit http://www.kenhayashi.com

978-0-595-28080-3
0-595-28080-3

Lightning Source UK Ltd.
Milton Keynes UK
06 September 2009

143396UK00001B/162/A